STOP, DROP,

& ROLL

Life changing tools for success!

Valerie! Step into your greatness!

Stop, Drop, and Roll

Life changing tools for success!

Lena Cohen

© 2016 by Lena Cohen

All rights reserved

Cover Work:

Photography: Serge Fils-Aime

Graphics/Production: Gary Robinson of LogoGlo

ISBN-13:978-1542347938
ISBN-10:1542347939

For Myla, Aziyah, and Noel

You little ladies inspire me to be all that I can possibly be in this world. I strive to be someone you all can always look up to, admire, and love. Never let go of your dreams, no matter what. Shoot for the stars, and know that you were created for a purpose in this world. You can do, be, and have whatever your sweet little heart's desire. Just remember to always put God first and walk in the light. I love you girls; dream big!

"For I know the plans I have for you," declares the Lord, "plans to prosper you and not to harm you, plans to give you hope and a future."
—Jeremiah 29:11

Contents

Preface
Acknowledgments
Introduction

Chapter 1 So, Who Am I?	1
Chapter 2 Stop Procrastinating!	9
Chapter 3 Drop the Negativity	47
Chapter 4 Drop Negative People	68
Chapter 5 Drop the Old You!	96
Chapter 6 Drop Negative Places	104
Chapter 7 Drop Negative Things	124
Chapter 8 Change	132
Chapter 9 Roll with the Punches	142

Chapter 10 What Do You Believe?	155
Chapter 11 Learning to Connect	164
Chapter 12 Brilliant Resilience	182

Preface
>I wrote this book for people who are ready for change! Not just any kind of change though, the kind of positive change that shifts your world, changes your perspective, and thrusts you into a new universe. The kind of change that makes you unrecognizable to your family and friends. If you are ready for that kind of change, if you are ready to make all of your dreams come true, then I welcome you. I welcome you to come on this journey with me, to find the new you

>I created this book to be interactive. Just me and you; talking, sharing and growing. So, when I ask questions, I want you to really stop and think. Where there are lines, fill them in. Where there are worksheets, do the work. I want you to commit to being a different person after reading this book, to really take it all in. I want you to be prepared to take on the world and whatever it has for you once you're finished reading this book. I hope and pray that you have progressed toward optimal peace and happiness upon completion. It's all about taking a risk to do something different from what you've been doing and to do it consistently! This will result in a completely different lifestyle; and trust me—it's worth the risk.

>I hope that you will also experience a spiritual shift after reading this book. You will see me use the terms God or the universe along with prayer and meditation. This happens to be my faith and belief system of choice. But my goal is to reach people of all different backgrounds and

nationalities. So, be assured that the tools in this book can be applied to whomever you praise and however you pray. I want to help you establish a stronger spiritual connection and faith system. Without that, we are lost; we are without peace and fulfillment. I believe that I was created in the likeness of my higher power, so I aim to live the life that God has called me for. I know the greatness of my God, because I have experienced it. The Bible says, "Now to him who is able to do exceedingly abundantly above all that we ask or think, according to the power that works in us" (Ephesians 3:20). We have "the power within us" to reach our highest potential for greatness. It's up to you to manifest it.

Acknowledgments

Adrian
Thank you for your constant love, support, affection, and friendship. Thank you for believing in me when I didn't believe in myself and for pushing me every step of the way. I'm so incredibly blessed to be in such a caring union with someone who also happens to be my best friend.
I love you!

Melissa
You've been a phenomenal cousin, sister, friend, therapist, mediator, event coordinator, and true confidante. You're an amazing woman, and it has truly been a pleasure growing up with you as my shero!

Mom
Because of you, I am!

Introduction

Start by doing what's necessary; then do what's possible; and suddenly you are doing the impossible.
—Francis of Assisi

     Greatness lies within you. It's just a matter of how deep you're willing to dig to find it. There's an unlimited amount of untapped potential flowing through your heart, your mind, and your spirit just waiting to be released so that you may rise to the next level. You possess talent and skills that you haven't even begun to discover yet, because it's in growth that you will find true enlightenment. It's in growth that we discover unbounded possibilities, but you must be at liberty to grow—free from fear, uncertainty, and worry. The key to achieving this greatness is to never underestimate the power you have within you.

     You have what it takes. There's no situation, no difficulty, and no pain too great for you to bear. If there's one thing I know for sure, it's that on this journey you will face obstacles, disappointments, and doubt. It matters not how or when, because true enlightenment lives in the why. Why are you facing this difficulty? What are you to gain from this experience? What lessons are here for you to learn? Who are you supposed to be as a result of this? Every event that occurs in our lives is custom designed for us. It's up to you to fight for that person on the other side of the growth or difficulty!

I promise—you will be impressed with the new you.

You must believe deep down in your heart that you were created for a divine purpose. You can't be afraid to go on the journey of seeking the truth of why you're here. I promise that you were sent to this earth as a gift, as light, and as love. Be mindful of that! Be cautious of the words you speak, the actions you take, and the beliefs you stand for. Be cautious of the lasting impressions that you will leave on others. Be the gift that you were meant to be. Discover your purpose.

There is a higher power that dwells deep inside of you, and because you are so magnificent in who you are, the universe takes residence in you so that it may be expressed to the world. Take heed of that invaluable fact, knowing the worth of your mental, physical, and spiritual self. Feed your body and your mind only what will nurture, cleanse, and stimulate growth. Accomplish these adorning tasks with love, respect, and constant affection for who you are. Be in love with you, the person you are today! Love and treat yourself with great pride, understanding the great value you bring to this world.

And, above all, live brilliantly! Bless everything and everyone you touch. Even in your dark moments, exude what I like to call "brilliant resilience." Learn, grow, and become even better than you were before, but do so in a way that shines and inspires others. Show them what true purpose looks like, because with it, nothing can stop you.

1
So, Who Am I?

I am a product of Camden, New Jersey, which happens to be one of the most impoverished, violent, and dangerous communities in our country. I grew up as the only child in a single-parent household, with a mother who once relied on the government for financial assistance. I was a college dropout. I made a lot of bad decisions—like, a lot! I've made enough mistakes to last a lifetime, some that led me down the wrong path. I am a woman who has been denied, broken, hurt, abused, scorned, abandoned, and lied to. I have been physically, emotionally, mentally, sexually, and verbally abused. I'm a person who has suffered death time and time again, losing loved one after loved one. At one point, I was a person who lost faith, and I gave up all hope for a better future. I was on the verge of letting it all go. I've suffered depression, and there were times when things were so dark for me that I contemplated suicide. I was unhappy, unfulfilled, afraid, and felt invisible at times.

About seven years ago, though, when I was at my lowest point, I learned how to co-create with God in order to create the life I desired. I moved toward healing and learned how to love myself. So, who am I today? I am the woman I set out to be, the woman I intended on being, and the woman God would have me to be. I am a college graduate with two degrees, and hoping to get my doctorate one day. A lot of people know me through my work at the Boys & Girls Club, as an advocate or Youth of the Year recipient. Some know me from my work in television and production; on one of the top syndicated news-magazine shows in the country. Others may have seen my TED Women 2016 video or heard me speak at a conference. I've done a lot of my empowerment work through my first company, *You're Beautiful Honie* and my non-profit *Women Operating in Opulence*. I also provide counseling to foster children and their families in hopes of making their transition process smoother. But for those of you who don't know me, welcome! I appreciate you coming on this journey with me.

Although I've been recognized locally and nationally for my work as a CEO, community activist, and coach, which is a true honor, there's so much more to who I am. I'm healed, in love, free, happy, and a dignified child of God. To call me a dreamer would be an understatement. I'm constantly searching for ways to achieve greatness. I simply want to be better today than I was yesterday—a better friend, a better lover, a better team player, a better member of my family and community, a better partner, and a better source of energy for everyone around me. I never give up, and I always give it my all. I've come a long way, but I'm still learning. In so many ways, I'm just like you…still trying to figure it all out. That transition from hurt, broke, and beat down to healed, free, and living life to the fullest didn't happen overnight. I'm still learning, growing, and changing.

Sometimes we fail to realize that we're all human—that none of us asked to be born and that we are all here just trying to make it. Most of us are all striving for the same thing. To be loved, to have security, to be happy, and to be healthy—to live freely! But what creates that happiness and freedom is totally different for each and every one of us. We're all striving for it nonetheless—for peace and contentment in our lives. Despite our valiant efforts to maintain that peace and contentment, we will still see tragedy, defeat, and pain. The glory is found when we learn how to enjoy life regardless and take pleasure in the gift of experience. It is found when we no longer hold on to the pain but release it and learn from it. I don't know it all, but I know enough. I know enough to thank God each day and make happiness my number-one priority and choice. I know that my path, whether good or bad, was custom built to make me the woman that I am today, and I appreciate it. I learned to appreciate my trials, to learn from them, and to understand that I'm not the only one going through something.

    If you are reading this, it means that somewhere in your life, you want things to change. I'm ready to take your hand and say, "Let's do it together!" There are very few emotions that I haven't experienced in my life. I can almost guarantee, that whatever it is you're going through, I've been there in some way, shape, or form. My life experiences have taught me more than any professor of any college could ever teach me. I'm going to share a lot of those experiences with you, because I want you to understand that you can maneuver through this world no matter what situation comes your way.

Just think, I've been molested on numerous occasions as a child, sexually assaulted as a teen, grew up without my father, gave up a full scholarship to my first choice school, suffered five deaths in one year, dropped out of my second choice school, dropped in to an abusive relationship with an alcoholic, left him and dated someone who mentally and emotionally abused me for four years.... and I'm still here! That's my past. If I can move past my pain, I promise, you can too. I look forward to providing you with the tools and treasures that granted me access to an entirely new life.

What I Want You to Take from This Book
One of the most controversial topics I hit on in my workshops is "Why and how you got to this place in your life." I ask people to repeat the phrase "I am where I am because of the thoughts, actions, choices, and decisions of my past." Sometimes it's extremely difficult for people to get through this. I realize that some of you were just dealt a bad hand, and somehow, someway, you're just trying to play it accordingly. Then there are others, myself included, that have no trouble messing up their own lives all by themselves by creating their own problems unnecessarily, feeding their vices, and simply not doing the right thing. The great thing about life is that you can always start over. Once you finally admit and acknowledge your part in where you are, you can move forward. You have the power to create a totally new existence for yourself, if you choose to.

My entire life changed once I decided it was going to change. You have the capability to do, be, have, and achieve anything and to go anywhere you want in this world, but you have to believe in yourself enough to do so. That's so cliché, right? Wrong! It's not cliché. It is the truth—a fact! You just have to want it badly enough. You have to want change more than anything else in this world. You have to find your breaking point, your passion, and your motivation. Without it, you probably won't have the drive to do any of the things you really want to do in life or live the life you really want to live. If you are waiting for someone else's help, financial support, love, encouragement, or handout in order to follow your dreams or change your life, you might as well pack it up now—because you'll always be waiting. Change starts with you making the decision that you won't be a victim, won't be poor, won't be overweight, won't be single, won't be unhappy, and that you will live up to your highest potential. You are the only one that can make that decision.

It all starts with you. You have so much power in your thoughts and in your words, but you may have no idea how to use them for your benefit. Before you can set goals and take action, you have to be mentally ready to succeed. You have to learn how to control your mind, your thoughts, and your emotions. You have to start removing the negative thoughts of self-doubt, fear, and anxiety. Learn how to uplift yourself, read more positive works, listen to spiritually uplifting music, attend a yoga class, or learn how to meditate. Start doing things that are conducive to a positive state of mind. Once you decide to have a positive, happy, joy-filled life, all the energy around you will change, but you must be putting that energy out for the world to receive it.

Along with being in a positive place mentally, you need speak positivity into your world. Stop saying, "I can't, I don't, I'm not," and "If only." The more you think it and speak it, the more you believe it. And once you believe it—trust me—it will begin to manifest in your life. It's up to you whether you want more positive things or negative things to show up in your life. These are choices and decisions that you have to make, but I want to help you get there.

When I decided I was going to change my life, the universe opened up for me. God opened windows where doors had been slammed in my face. He moved mountains when I had no energy left to climb. He placed angels in my life for guidance and protection when he knew the devil would be working against me. My spiritual relationship became the most important relationship in my life. As long as I was walking on the right path, I had nothing to worry about and surely nothing to fear. So, as you go along this journey, remember that faith will eliminate fear. If you are still scared, anxious, or fearful, you need to build your faith. Don't worry, I'm going to share some of the techniques I use to build my spiritual core with you later.

Why I Decided to Write This Book
So many people began to ask me what my lightbulb moment was. How did I get out of my fog? How did I overcome grief and depression? How did I regain my confidence as a woman? How did I have the strength to leave that relationship? How did I start the healing process? Where did I find the motivation and will? What restored my faith? How did I literally change my whole entire life? How did success come so quickly for me? Everyone wanted to know how I survived all the distress. They wanted to know what my breaking point was and how I was able to overcome the hardship. To be honest, there are no simple answers to all of these questions. It wasn't just one thing or another that began the process, it was a culmination of numerous events that had taken place over my lifetime. The healing process didn't happen instantaneously, I've been on this journey toward greatness for the past seven years.

But if I had to choose one moment in time, the catalyst to my journey, it would be the day my romantic relationship became physically abusive. I would compare my life, then, to that of a fire—there was a spark, then flames, total meltdown, suffocation, heat, smoke, premonitions, the sight of everything I worked for destroyed, a feeling of total hopelessness. I think we all have these unexplainable moments where we feel like our world is crashing, burning down to the ground. A key moment of distress that seems to rock our world, something that change the entire makeup of our existence. Sometimes these moments or events become scars that never heal properly, altering our character. There're only two things you can do in response: you can stand there and allow your entire life to burn and crumble to the ground, taking you along with it, or you can *Stop, Drop, and Roll;* get up, get out of the fire, build a new home, and a new life. I'm here to help you build that new life, get acclimated, and enjoy the next level. So please forgive me in advance if I don't "sugar coat" things. My life wasn't sugar coated, and the people, conversations, and experiences that pushed me toward greatness weren't either. I want to give you my best; so I'm going to be brutally honest and upfront with you the whole way through.

2
Stop Procrastinating!
Create a Sense of Urgency in Your Life

The Heat

Everyone has moments in their lives when the smoke detector goes off (when they've reached their breaking point). You realize that you're not happy and something's wrong. Deep down inside you know you should make a move. But you stand there, looking around, assessing the situation, assuming you have time because the flames haven't engulfed your home yet. So what do you do? Instead of saving your life, you procrastinate. You start trying deciphering what's important—what you can salvage. You begin to run around your house picking and choosing the things you will save. Now you're being weighed down by all of these things, instead of just getting up and getting out of the fire; not realizing that you can't carry it all—you are enough. Just you: you are the most important and the most valuable thing in this fire. You've got to be willing to work with what you have and face what's next, even if it's just you by yourself. The heat is starting to overwhelm you, and the flames are getting closer. But you can't make up your mind about what you'd like to leave behind. You waste time contemplating finances—how will you rebuild—and start getting emotional about past memories you created in the house. You cry hopelessly about losing the life you had instead of getting up and getting out of the fire and becoming excited about the life you can create ahead—a better life, a new life, the life you deserve. At some point, it hits you! The heat rises, and it begins to swelter. It's blistering now, and you realize there's no place to go but out.

It's a Fire! Stop Procrastinating! Get Out Now!

What is the true reason behind your procrastination? Why are you putting off imperative work that could change your life forever? Is it the fear of the unknown? Do you avoid doing things because you don't know what the outcome will be? Are you afraid of what people will think or say about you? Do you feel inadequate? Are you waiting for the right time, the right opportunity, or the right person? What is it that keeps you from creating movement and action in your life? Is it a lack of passion? Are you holding on to the past? Are you afraid of facing emotions and tapping into deep, dark places that are holding you back from living a life fulfilled? This was me! I have experienced all of these things. But we have to recognize which of these actions and feelings are valid and which of them aren't.

    The first step to overcoming procrastination is transparency and honesty with yourself. Self-awareness is essential to growth. You must be aware of your own demons and character flaws before you can prepare to fight them. Ask yourself, "When I know something has to be done, why do I put it off?" There's usually something deeper, something more than just laziness. There are reasons why we avoid challenges and changes in our lives. There are deeper reasons to why we say we'll do it tomorrow or put off the most important things on our to-do list. There are reasons why we simply let our hopes and dreams for a better life fall by the wayside. Let's explore some of the reasons I procrastinated and some of the things that held me back that may be holding you back as well.

Not Holding Yourself Accountable
Mistakes show us what we need to learn.
—Peter McWilliams

Self-awareness is one of the greatest things you can strive for in life. I know that being open and honest with yourself is not always the easiest thing to do. More often than not, we create the problems in our lives. Most of us, however, like to point the finger at someone or something else. It's our parents, our spouses, our kids, or our bosses who create all the problems in our lives. At some point, you have to take a long look in the mirror and ask yourselves, "What role have I played in creating this situation?"

While at my breaking point, I had to really accept the fact that my ex was bad news. I knew he was abusive, and I knew he drank in excess. I knew! But for some reason, I guess I thought I was different. I thought I could help him change. I thought that if I sent him to rehab, all our issues would be solved. I had to accept the truth in order to move forward. I saw the red flags, but I continued to ignore them or make excuses for why I couldn't leave. He "needed" me. I kept him on track. He would fall apart without me, right? Wrong! I brought all that turmoil on myself. I know it's hard to hold yourself accountable. It was much easier for me to say, "Oh, it's not his fault—his father was an alcoholic," or "He's dealing with a lot, and he just wants to unwind when he gets home."

I had to wake up and realize that if I didn't acknowledge my part in whatever happened, I could never change my reality. How can you change something you don't feel like you have control over? How can you begin to solve a problem, if you don't admit you have one? As hard as it may be, we all must acknowledge where we're creating, allowing, or accepting some of the challenges in our lives. It's important to be honest with yourself first. We all have an internal moral compass that lets us know when something isn't right. Learn how to tap into that and acknowledge where you can begin to create change in your life to make it better. You hold the ultimate power in changing your world.

Where in your life do you think you could hold yourself more accountable for your actions and decisions? Write down the top three issues in your life, and be honest with yourself about the role you've played in the situation. Once you've done that begin to write down and explore the things *you* can do to change.

You're Too Comfortable
God, make me so uncomfortable that I will do the very thing I fear.
—Ruby Dee

There was a time when I thought I had an established career in finance. Oh, how naive of me! I got my first real job when I sixteen as a bank teller. By nineteen I was a teller manager, and at twenty-one, I went into retirement planning. It was all I knew, so I thought it was what I was supposed to be doing. I was good at it, I liked working with the people in my community, and I didn't really need my degree to be successful in doing so. I had several licenses and the access to obtain any additional ones I needed to grow in the industry. I was beginning to make lump sums of money like I had never seen before. I had my own place, a car, and I was taking care of myself. What did I need to go back to school for? My bills were paid, I traveled when I wanted to (although my idea of traveling then is completely different from my idea of traveling now), I had a decent wardrobe, and I wasn't starving. What more could I want, right?

Wrong! Being comfortable, just existing, or allowing life to control you should never be the goal. There is always more to learn and a bountiful, more abundant life to live. You should always be seeking a deeper level of self. There's always a new level of spiritual growth, supernatural healing, purpose, passion, and overall fulfillment we should be moving toward. But at the time, I didn't know that. I didn't know that you could have a career doing something you actually loved to do. I didn't know that you could take your passions and create a life of freedom. I didn't know that my life had purpose, that I was here for a more divine reason. All I knew was that I was independent, and putting off college wasn't looking so bad.

Where there are no challenges, there is no growth. I learned more from being in uncomfortable situations than I ever did when I was comfortable. Making the decision to get up and challenge myself every day was key. There's glory in overcoming what seemed difficult, scary, or uncomfortable and turning it into a triumphant testimony. It's so rewarding pushing through, and being able to say, "I did it!" You'll be surprised at what you can do, and what you can accomplish when you challenge yourself. Get out of your comfort zone and create some big, audacious goals for yourself. All the greats have said get comfortable with being uncomfortable. It gets easier—I promise you. Once you take the leap of faith and achieve one victory outside of your comfort zone, the confidence will come. The more you do things for the first time, the more comfortable you will be with taking risks. Greatness lies outside of your comfort zone. Make a move, get up, take a leap, and do something different. Challenge yourself today.

What situation are you too comfortable in? How can you challenge yourself and get out of your comfort zone today to create a better tomorrow? Where do you need to stop procrastinating and take a leap of faith in your life?

Fear of the Unknown
Leap, and the net will appear.
—John Burroughs

Sometimes we procrastinate because we don't know what's up ahead. We put off committing to something because we're not exactly sure how it will affect the outcome of our situation. Why does knowing make us comfortable by nature? Why don't you trust yourself enough to know you can handle whatever comes your way? Why don't you believe that if you have faith, do the right thing, and proceed with confidence, everything will work out for the best? Because guess what? There's no such thing as certainty. Even when you think you know something for sure, there is a chance of the unforeseen happening. Sometimes life just comes out of nowhere and shifts your whole being. Even when you have your life all mapped out, and you think you have everything in order, things don't always go as planned.

    You don't always have to know what's coming to feel safe and secure. You already have a track record for overcoming the unknown. You never knew what the first day of school would bring, but you gained new friends, learned new material, and created lasting memories. Maybe you even found a special person you liked. You might have also struggled in a few subjects, endured some people who weren't nice to you, and put up with some teachers you didn't like —but you made it through. Maybe, the first day on your new job seemed like it would never end. Next thing you know it's your ten-year anniversary. Three promotions and several lateral transitions later, here you are. You didn't know what being a parent would be like, but you knew that protecting, providing for, and loving that child would be a great start. You took everything else day by day. I've seen people read every book and go to every class, stressing themselves out about not knowing what's to come as a parent. Some things just come with experience. You won't know or understand how to deal with it until the baby gets here. Most things in life are learned through experience. There's no magic secret to perfecting life. You just live it!

You might *think* you have to know everything before making a huge life decision, but you don't. You just have to have a little bit of faith! Having faith beyond what you can see is one of the greatest gifts you can possess. I always say, "Strengthen your faith, and your fears will subside." I live by Jeremiah 29:11, "'For I know the plans I have for you,' declares the Lord, 'plans to prosper you and not to harm you, plans to give you hope and a future.'" These words give me comfort. I know that whatever direction I'm headed in, as long as I put God first in all I do, there's nothing to fear about what's to come. His plans are to prosper me, not to harm me.

Why are you fearful of the unknown? What areas of your life are you avoiding because of fear? What can you do today to strengthen your self-esteem and trust yourself more when it comes to making decisions about the here and now?

Lack of Passion
Passion is energy. Feel the power that comes from focusing on what excites you.
—Oprah Winfrey

Maybe you are procrastinating because you simply don't want to do whatever the task at hand is. If you are not doing something you love or trying to accomplish something that will fulfill you, I can almost promise that you won't be motivated to do so. When you set your mind to achieving something great, it should also be something that excites you, that gets your heart pumping, and that makes you feel alive. If you aren't the least bit interested in the task you're trying to accomplish, your drive will eventually begin to fade. You can't choose to do something because your parents have always wanted you to do it. You can't choose a career based on the latest projections in the career-builder magazine. You can't live a life based on what your spouse wants for you. You can't work for twenty years at a job that you just don't like. Well, technically, you can, and there are actually a lot of people that do —I was one of them. But when you do this, you sacrifice your happiness and overall quality of life. You waste precious time that you can never get back; years of your life just fade away. Every day is dull, uneventful, and lackluster. If it's not something you genuinely want to do or enjoy doing, nine times out of ten I can guarantee that you won't be happy doing it. You may be able to tolerate it, but who wants to live such an uninspiring life, just tolerating the things they do every day all day?

    You may be able to fool yourself for a while, but eventually you will feel a significant void in your life. Even though my bills were paid, I had my own place, a car, and lived relatively well considering where I came from, deep down inside I was unhappy. There was a silent emptiness in what I was doing. I spent eight years in a career that I fell into because of my first job as a teenager. It wasn't by choice. My heart wasn't in it. I didn't have a passion for finance. I just didn't know how to transition. I didn't know how to look for or find my passion.

    Don't live, just because. Don't marry, just because. Don't go to work at a place that makes you sick to your stomach every day, just because. Don't allow people in your life, just because. Don't buy that item on sale, just because. Don't do anything, just because. Be calculated! Do things because you honestly and truly want to do them. Do things because your heart skips a beat when you do them. Spend time with people who love you, who excite you, who make you better. Live a life of passion. Wake up! Live and feel what it's like to be alive. There are no do-overs in this lifetime. If you are not living and loving with passion, you are wasting not only your time but your life. One of the most important things I learned while sitting down every day with people who were sixty-five and older was to live life free of regret. You can't do that if you're not living life on your own terms. You don't want to wake up one day and say, "I wish I would have…I wish I could have…" What's the point of living this life if you aren't living it with passion? Take pride in having passion for yourself, your spouse, your kids, your career, your hobbies, your personal relationship with God, and simply the gift of life. Each and every day that you're here is a blessing. Wake up and find your passion for life!

    By all means, do what's best for you and your situation. I know we all have different circumstances, responsibilities, and burdens to carry. I know we can't all just pick up and do whatever it is that we want to do in life without regard for anyone or anything else. I understand that in life, we have to do what we must do so that someday we can do what we want to do. I get it, but life has also taught me that "someday" isn't promised. That "someday" you're waiting for—to be happy, to live, to be free, and to enjoy life—may not come. We have to live each day with our hearts open and with love, kindness, passion, and excitement.

What excites you? What make you happy? What causes or beliefs are you passionate about? What gives you hope to live for today? You have to find the answers to these questions! It's freeing. It's how I get through the most difficult times. When you understanding why you're fighting through life, that understanding gives you a stronger foundation and will to keep going in the darkest of times.

Fear of Failure or Success
In order to succeed, your desire for success should be greater than your fear of failure.
—Bill Cosby

I can't understand for the life of me why we have become so afraid of making mistakes when no one is perfect and everyone has had their fair share of fumbles. It's a part of growth and gaining experience. They say the difference between the master and the beginner is that the master has failed more times than the beginner has even tried! How powerful is that? Failure exists only when you give up. If you continue to push and to pursue your dreams, potential failure transforms into lessons, practical knowledge, experience, wisdom, and clarity; it transforms you into an expert in your field. Most often, failure leads to our greatest epiphanies in life. It tests our strength, but it builds our character. Sometimes I want to shake people and ask them, "Who do you think you are? Why do think you deserve a carefree, picture-perfect life without flaws?" I mean, really, how can you expect to learn anything from life without experiencing some sort of challenge? Who is expecting us to be perfect anyway? I don't know anyone who has lived a mistake-free, flawless life. Do you?

    Michael Jordan said, "I can accept failure; everyone fails at something. But I can't accept not trying." Putting something off, procrastinating, or not trying something day after day, year after year because you are afraid to fail is cowardly. Face life fearlessly. Have a little chutzpah! So what if you fail? We all do! Just take a second and think about the good that failing could actually do for your life. After failing, many have gone on to flourish, succeed, and shine. Greatness is upon you. Don't focus on your shortcomings or your weaknesses. Focus on your strengths and skills. Failing only adds credibility and texture to your journey. Otherwise I'd be suspicious about how you made it to the top without making one mistake.

    You are not alone. We have all faced the fear of failure. Little did I know my fear wasn't failure it was success. Growing up in Camden, in a single-parent household, I didn't really know what success looked like. My mother didn't explain to me what I was "supposed" to be striving toward.

I'm the first in my immediate family to achieve the level of education and success that I have, so I didn't have a lot of examples of the path that resembles the one I'm on now. My understanding and idea of success came from my environment, the media, and simple assumptions. I had a totally distorted view of success and how to obtain it. Street success came with jail time, remorse, and/or death. Being an athlete or celebrity came with public pressure, ridicule, and lack of privacy. I grew up thinking business men, high-level executives, and CEOs were all sharks, preying on the innocent and taking advantage of the system. Local small-business owners always looked like they'd do anything to breathe again because their businesses were drowning. I thought the only people with success were those who inherited it, took advantage of the next man to get it, hit the lottery, or participated in some kind of criminal activity. My view of what success was and how to get it was warped.

Not only was I afraid of who success would turn me into, but I was also afraid of the weight it would put on my shoulders. When you begin to stand out, shine, or prove to be a leader, things change and people change. Everything changes! Very early, I became an ambassador for my community. I have been telling my story, talking about my experiences, and mentoring for over ten years now. At the young age of seventeen, I was the Boys & Girls Club of Camden County's Youth of the Year. I wasn't afraid of losing—I was afraid of winning. With each triumph in my life, all I could think about was what's next. What will they want from me? What will they expect of me? Am I ready? Will I measure up? More people will be watching. Young girls will be relying on me. My mistakes will be publicized. With each level of success, the fear got stronger. I found myself sabotaging things in my life because I wasn't 100 percent sure I was ready. I had to tell myself to stop—to stop overthinking things and to stop overanalyzing situations that hadn't even happened yet. I had to tell myself to just do it, just live my life unapologetically. I had to tell myself that I was sufficient and capable of handling life and all that comes with it. I had to retrain my thought process. Don't ever question or doubt yourself. If I can change my ideas about fear, failure, and success so can you. You are already a success, so there's nothing to fear!

    I met Judy Smith at a conference a few years ago, and she gave me a good talking-to that brought me to tears. Judy Smith's life is loosely portrayed on the ABC hit show Scandal. She is the real-life Olivia Pope. I spoke to her about my fears of reaching the next level, how I may not be ready, how each leap I take seems to get bigger and harder to take, and how I was beginning to feel the pressure of success. She replied, "You are sufficient!" She told me that I already had everything I needed. See, we are all custom built with exactly what we need to succeed, but we don't realize it. Along the way, I had to understand that there is absolutely no reason to be afraid, because I belong at the top! Half the time we are convincing ourselves that we're not ready for success when, in fact, we are! So don't be afraid of failing, and don't be afraid of succeeding either—you're ready! Everything you've ever wanted is already yours, and you are beyond deserving. It's about you getting up, getting out of the fire, and going to get it —today, without procrastinating!

What is it that you are really afraid of, and how long are you willing to allow that fear to hold you back from truly living? You have an amazing life waiting for you. How long are you going to allow the fear of failure hold you back from experiencing all you deserve?

Waiting for the Right Time
Lord, remind me how brief my time on earth will be. Remind me that my days are numbered, and that my life is fleeing away.
—Psalm 39:4

How many times have you heard, "Life is short?" Like, a million times, right? Ask yourself, "How many times do I have to hear it to fully understand and operate in it?" How many times must you be told that time waits for no man and that tomorrow isn't promised to any of us? How many times must you be told there is no such thing as "the perfect time" or "getting your ducks all in a row"? Maybe you're one of those people who believes that all the stars have to align just perfectly before you can act on your dreams. Well, I'm here to tell you that it doesn't work like that. I can't tell you how many times I've listened to people's excuses when it comes to time. Waiting and waiting and waiting—procrastination is just another form of avoidance, fear, and laziness. It's an excuse to put off important things that could change your life forever.

We overestimate the time we have on this earth and underestimate the time it takes to realistically accomplish our goals. I have lost so many people, young and old, whom I loved dearly. Experiencing all of these deaths was horrible, but losing someone young always hits me where it hurts the most. I have lost five people close to me who were between the ages of sixteen and thirty. Most recently, I lost one of my best friends. He was my high-school sweetheart. As we grew into adulthood we mutually agreed that a relationship wasn't in our future, but we remained extremely close for over fourteen years. Our families are well respected and loved by one other. There was nothing that could break our bond. We experienced a lot together over the years and guided each other through many of life's tragedies, until one day he just didn't wake up. That was it. At first there was no explanation—a clean autopsy. He was healthy and strong; it was a heartbreaking tragedy for all of us. For months, we had no answers. Later they found it was his heart.

His death taught me so much—more than I could have ever imagined. But one of the most important lessons I learned from him was to do your best and live up to your potential while you're here on earth. Although he was only here for thirty short years, I feel like he had a lifetime of wisdom. It was as though he'd been here before—he just understood it all. He lived life as though he knew something the rest of us didn't know. After his death, I found myself asking questions like: What am I doing with my time? How do I live my life? What legacy will I leave? How do I love? How do I treat people? Would I chase my dreams differently if I knew how much time I had left? Would I walk with a greater stride toward my purpose if I knew I only had two years to live? Would the little things bother me as much? His death changed me and my outlook on life. I became less concerned with the minor trials of living and became fully committed to focusing on what really mattered in my world, which was my purpose. He was here for a reason, so am I, and so are you!

Stop procrastinating, and create a sense of urgency in your life. Live for today, be happy today, connect with God today, forgive today, love today, and free yourself today. What are you waiting for and why? What's holding you back from capitalizing on where you are in life right now? Time is a figment of your imagination, live for this moment right now; and work to leave a legacy to be proud of.

Life Happened, and You're Overwhelmed
In tragedy, find your lesson. It is then you triumph!
—Lena Cohen

We are all subject to this thing called life. Unfortunately, there's no way around it. You may experience disappointment, heartbreak, financial struggles, family ordeals, health issues, grief, pain, and other tragedies—that's life. I don't know anyone who's exempt. That's just a part of being alive here on earth. Once you realize that things happen and you're not exempt, handling challenges gets easier. The shock factor will subside, and it'll take the whole woe-is-me sting out of everyday life situations. You're not the only one who is depressed. You're not the only one whose parents abandoned them. You're not the only one who has struggled to provide for their family. You're not the only one who has been beaten down, broken, abused, and taken advantage of. You have a choice to make. Will you allow your struggle to turn your whole life into an awful story of tragedy, or will your struggle be a tragic moment in an amazing story of triumph? It's never about what happens to you—it's all about how you respond to it.

    The fact is, regardless of your background, ethnicity, class, gender, or race, you may suffer some type of distress in life. If you are waiting for your life to be perfect to chase your dreams or make something of yourself, you are wasting your time. If you are procrastinating because you are overwhelmed with life and all the drama that comes with it, you'll never get anything done. I'm always pushing through, pressing on in spite of, working hard through the worst of times, and putting on a smile even though things are falling apart behind the scenes; believe me my life isn't perfect. There's no pause button on life. You can't stop life events so you can achieve success. You have to dig deep and find the strength to carry on no matter what. These life challenges come with something mighty and great though! They come with character, experience, and wisdom. Why would you let life beat you down for nothing, when there's something to gain from pushing through? For every difficulty I have experienced, I've learned a much needed lesson. Don't let these experiences happen in vain. Take all that you can from each and every experience you fight through.

  Don't get me wrong, I know that there are some instances where pushing through seems to be impossible—great tragedy and unspeakable pain. The type of pain that requires a supernatural healing. The key here is to take your time, recover, and prioritize. Take the time you need to handle your mental, emotional, and spiritual health. Doing so is essential. We all have goals and things we want to achieve, but when your heart, mind, and spirit are broken it's hard —I know. You must find time for resolve. However, it's important that you identify how long that time will be. Being closed off to the world or isolating yourself for long periods of time can be dangerous. I've been there, and it's not fun. It's dark and can sometimes be dangerous. Take the time you need, but use that time to focus on healing. I went years without getting the therapy I needed, and during times of extreme stress or pressure, those unresolved emotions always came back to haunt me. You can't run from the pain forever. In times of stress, all those bottled-up emotions are just waiting to erupt; which can cause a mental, emotional, or physical breakdown. If you don't get the appropriate help, things will continue to get worse.

The importance of mental and emotional health is something we don't talk about enough in our society. I know so many people who are carrying heavy burdens, and they just don't know how to release them. Depression is a serious disorder that can cause serious damage if left untreated. If life's difficulties are becoming too overwhelming for you, it's okay to put things on hold, take care of yourself first, and recover. Recover, recover, recover. Certain things from our past can weigh heavy on us and keep us from achieving our greatest potential, if we let them. You will remain paralyzed in your current situation if you do not seek healing or help with the challenges and difficulties that have hindered you the most. After you have taken a designated amount of time to recover, heal or to learn how to cope with a devastating event, it's important to prioritize. You don't have to accomplish everything at once. Take your time, and figure out what pieces of the puzzle to life you'd like to put back together first. Be honest about what areas of your life need the most help, and never be afraid to ask for that help if you need it.

  Don't allow your past or current circumstances dictate your life. You were placed on this earth for a reason. Tap into that reason. Find your passion, and push through. You are the gift. There's no shame in admitted your hurt, the shame comes from living in it! We all get overwhelmed; just make sure you take the time you need to recover. Begin prioritizing and put together a succession plan that will benefit your future self.

You Don't Have the Money or Resources
Ya gots to work with what you gots to work with.
—Stevie Wonder

You don't have what you need to succeed right? What's new? When I look at our society, the middle class seems to be disappearing, creating the haves and the have-nots. Even if you have more than what you had before, you'd still say you don't have enough. In our culture, we're never satisfied, and we're always searching for more. No matter how good we have it, we feel like it's not enough. Well, guess what? Sometimes you have to work with what you have. Be resourceful, get creative, connect with other people in your field, and learn how to be more innovative. That creativity and innovation will be what sets you apart from so many others. Those who have the money aren't forced to think outside the box. They resort to known options, services, and cookie-cutter templates. Those who may not have a disposable income are forced to come up with ideas that work for them. I love watching Shark Tank because I'm always amazed at the stories of people who were challenged financially and created a thriving business as a result of it. Challenges breed champions.

Stop being so afraid to be different, to be you. Be proud of who you are and where you are in your life. Be confident in who you're going to be, while remaining proud of who you are. Don't rush your success. With each stage, you'll learn new things and obtain new experiences that will prepare you for the next stage. If someone waved a magic wand over your life right now and gave you all the money and resources you needed to succeed, how confident would you be in utilizing all those resources? Would you even know how to use the money? Would you know who to trust? Would you know what moves to make in order to excel? How many times do we hear stories of people winning the lottery who are broke a few years later? Be willing to work through the process and learn at each stage.

Money doesn't create talent or experience. I love watching amateur chef competitions, because money doesn't change the ingredients. Flour, butter, sugar, and eggs are flour, butter, sugar, and eggs no matter what. The talent to transform those ingredients is up to the chef. All the ingredients are the same. As a chef, maybe you stood in the kitchen and watched your father, who was a disabled veteran and cooked all over the world; maybe your grandmother gave you a secret family recipe before she died; maybe you stayed after school looking at cookbooks in the library; or maybe you found a special way of prepping that is unorthodox due to your lack of resources. Tap into your unique *story*, love it, develop it and take pride in it. That's your moneymaker right there. Your gifts, your talents, who you are, and what you've been through, that's what makes you special. That's where you will find the key to your success. It's in the story—*your story*! People love supporting individuals that have an amazing story, someone they can relate to, that worked hard and earned it.

Why do people feel like they don't have to work for anything anymore? Yes, things can come with ease if you believe that they can, but you still have to put in the effort. Success isn't going to fall from the sky. If you don't have the money, then what do you do? Are you just going to give up on your dreams? I didn't have the money, but I had the will, faith, and grit. I worked hard, educated myself, and aligned myself with great people. I made it happen. If you don't have a computer, get a library card. If you don't have a car, catch the bus. There is absolutely no excuse for people to say they don't have the resources. We have the internet for Christ sakes. I didn't know the first thing about applying for tax-exempt status to get my nonprofit up and running, but I learned. My VP of operations (aka my best friend) and I did the research, we had conference calls that lasted for hours, we stayed up late figuring it out, we went online and downloaded every resource we could find from the IRS website and from several others. We followed a step-by-step guide we found, and—voilà! We did it and were approved within three months of applying. We were able to save up to ten thousand dollars by not hiring a lawyer. We were confident in our knowledge and we were resourceful. Most importantly, we had faith in each other, we knew each of us would stop at nothing to get it done, we had confidence in ourselves as individuals, and we were passionate about the cause. We held each other accountable, we got out of our comfort zones, we were fearless, we leaped with faith, and we worked together as a team! We weren't focused on what we *didn't* have, only on what we *did*.

Be inspired by where you are going! Focus on what you do have and what you can do. What can you work with right now to make your dreams come true? Break your goals down into smaller, more realistic steps so you can gain traction and excitement for achieving the things you want without having all the things you think you need. What gifts, talents, and experience do you have that can help you further your endeavors? Do you currently surround yourself with people who can help you achieve your dreams? If not, how can you position yourself better and surround yourself with people who do have the resources or will to help you get them?

Laziness
You can't complain about the results you didn't get from the hard work you didn't do.
—Mike Krzyzewski

Many of you simply aren't putting in the work—period! You just aren't motivated, you don't have the passion, and you'd rather take the easy way out. Yes, I hate getting up in the morning. I don't know why—I just do. I would love to get up whenever my body feels like telling me to get up, but to obtain the lifestyle I strive for, I know I have to get up and put in the work. Nobody is going to hand me anything. You have to wake up, get up, and get on with your life! It's not going to happen on its own. You have to put in the time, effort, and energy. You're going to get out of this life exactly what you put in to it. You have to create your own luck and make your own opportunities!

To my folks who do put in the work, don't confuse being tired and taking a break with being lazy. I am often exhausted from life. If I am beginning to feel overwhelmed by work, relationships, family, or life in general, I play hooky and take a "mental health day". I'll take some time to relax and get rejuvenated. This is not laziness. If you are putting in the work and need time out to take care of yourself, that's understandable. When I talk about laziness, I'm talking about the unwillingness to do something, not trying at all, and putting in no effort whatsoever to make something great happen in your life; procrastination on the highest level possible. I'm talking about the choice to be idle and slack off.

Remember, laziness only encourages more laziness. Once you switch gears and activate your plan, you will want to continue pursuing your goals. To activate! It means "to turn on, start up, get in motion, initiate, and get energized." A body in motion tends to stay in motion, while a body at rest tends to stay at rest. So let's get going!

Here are a few ways you can get going and battle laziness:
1. Put your health first.
    a. Are you getting enough sleep?
    b. Are you eating right?
    c. Are you working out?

        d. Are you getting all your daily vitamins and nutrients?
2. Visualize the life you want.
        a. Create a vision board.
        b. Go house hunting.
        c. Test-drive your dream car.
        d. Be inspired by the feeling of having what you want already.
3. Get an accountability partner—someone who can keep you on track. This person might be a
        a. Friend
        b. Spouse
        c. Coworker
        d. Life Coach or Mentor.
4. Be more strategic about scheduling your time and planning out your goals.
        a. Create new life habits by implementing a new daily schedule of things you need to do
        b. Give yourself deadlines with dates.
        c. Create SMART goals (Specific, Measurable, Achievable, Relevant, and Time bound).
5. Create positive affirmations that will prepare you mentally.
        a. I will use my time wisely.
        b. I will reach my highest potential.
        c. I will achieve all set goals.
        d. I am full of energy and life.
        e. I am ready for action.
6. Surround yourself with "movers and shakers."
        a. Be mindful and intentional about the people you allow in your life.

       b. Increase time spent with mentors, people who encourage and inspire you, and those who can motivate you to move forward.

       c. Learn from these people, take note of what they do, and feel their go-getter energy.

7. Set and achieve the smaller goals first.

       a. Break down your big goals into smaller, timely goals. (Once you achieve smaller goals, you will be much more confident.)

       b. Prioritize your goals.

       c. Prepare for discouragement. If/when you "fail" at achieving a goal, quickly recover, revise, and re-strategize. Don't sulk.

8. Avoid environments that promote laziness by creating a work space.

       a. Avoid the couch, your bedroom, and other cozy areas.

       b. Establish a place in your house where the work gets done.

       c. If you don't have an office, create one. Buy a small desk and place it in a corner of your living room. If you can't afford a desk, sit at the dining-room table. It's all about your mindset.

       d. Go to the local library or coffee shop to work if you need a physical environmental change to shift your mindset

9. Be self-aware. Take note of what you're doing and not doing.
    a. Sometimes, seeing what we're not accomplishing gives us a sense of conviction and accountability.
    b. Physically write down your goals, and make sure they are timely. Keep a calendar to help you stay on schedule.
    c. Have checkpoints for evaluations. Allow your accountability partner or coach to have a copy of the calendar or schedule so that they can do check-ins with you.
    d. You are more likely to accomplish your goals when you write them down. It also forces you to hold yourself accountable. Review, revise, re-strategize!
10. Reward yourself after you have finished your tasks or reached your goal.
    a. Give yourself something to look forward to.
    b. You can be lazy all you want on Saturday or Sunday if you've accomplished all that you intended to do during the week; pick a day of the week to be lazy, not every day of your life.
    c. If you put the time, energy, and work in, I see nothing wrong with a tangible reward at the end of an

accomplished goal. Go ahead and treat yourself.

Easily Distracted
You can always find a distraction if you're looking for one.
—Tom Kite

    In some cases, people aren't lazy and they don't intend to procrastinate—it just happens. They get distracted. They go to check their in-box and realize they have a Facebook notification. They go to check the Facebook notification and a friend messages them online, sending an invitation to chat. The friend sends a great video or tells them to go look at something on Instagram, and before they know it, they've wasted an hour and a half on social media. Then there are inquisitive folks, like me. We are diligently engulfed in an assignment, and suddenly there's a word, statement, or comment that grabs our attention. We need to know more, so we start googling and "YouTubing" until we know everything on that particular topic. This usually causes us to be off task for at least a half hour. Then, some of you have little people or big people to take care of, and just as you sit down to collect your thoughts, someone is crying or calling for you. I also encounter people who just can't focus, put the phone down, or refuse an opportunity to socialize. They reply to every text message, take every phone call, welcome people who just stop by, and take on every opportunity to hang out. They are always ready to share a few laughs, pour a few drinks, and hit the party; work can wait.

    As adults, most of the time we know what we have to do in order to be successful. It's all about implementing power habits. If you have to turn your phone off for an hour to work on your dreams, I promise you the world won't end. Don't sit in front of the television to read, write, or do work. Avoid the distraction altogether. Give yourself time limits. If you find yourself veering off course, give yourself five minutes to learn something new, and then it's back to work. If you have children, young or old, be open with them. If they are old enough to understand, let them know you need one hour of quiet time. Let them know the value of what you're doing. Tell them the benefits of your family's life changing. Explain the consequences of you not accomplishing your daily tasks. We don't give kids enough credit. They understand, and they want the best for you, just like you want the best for them. If you have young children, think about incorporating them into the project. Allow them to be a part of your dreams as well. Give them minor tasks or assignments. Ask them to draw mommy or daddy's logo, and give them (low-maintenance) crafts that make them feel like they're helping you. If you have unavoidable distractions, seek help. Western culture has brainwashed us into thinking we must do everything by ourselves, on our own, all the time. This type of thinking is so destructive! You are not alone, and you are not on this earth by yourself. Reach out, and take the hand of someone who can assist you.

When do you find yourself most distracted? Who or what can you avoid when trying to get something done? How can you prepare for and avoid these distractions? Who or what can help you with unavoidable distractions?

Lack of Focus
Never confuse motion with action.
—Benjamin Franklin

Distractions are one thing, but not being able to focus and execute is another. Lack of strategy and focus on a project will also keep you going in circles. Sometimes you want to accomplish a task, you have the energy to get it done, you have every intention of doing so, but you spread yourself too thin— exerting all that energy on multiple projects. Have you ever heard of a jack-of-all-trades, master of none? You start off strong with a great idea. You set up a great plan and you begin working, but then you gain passion in another area, leaving the last endeavor high and dry. You don't execute one set of plans before you move to the next. You do this every time you get to the heart of a project. Perhaps when things get tough, it's easier to just start something new than to face reality and push through. By all means, be a creator, an innovator, and a thought leader. That's great! I applaud you. Having said that, focus on one or two amazing ideas at a time. None of those amazing things will ever come to fruition if you always abandon them for the next amazing thing that comes along. You have to learn how to be fully committed to one idea at a time.

If you knew a person who claimed to be a personal trainer, that is a travel agent, who sells insurance, that has a plumbing company that does roofing and every year they ask to do your taxes, what exactly would you be *confident* that this person does? When I see people who are in multiple unrelated businesses I don't run to them for assistance in any area. You don't go to a dentist to get your heart checked and you wouldn't ask a painter to re-wire your house. It's important that you focus on one thing at a time and become an expert in your field when you're striving for that next level of success. Even in your personal life. It can be difficult to juggle five different life changing events at once. Could you imagine, transitioning from one field to another, going to school full-time, trying to expand your family, buy a new house, and become a vegan all at the same time?

If you'd really like to see yourself in a different position, if you really want to see change in your life, you have to be dedicated and give it your all. Don't give five things 20 percent; work on giving one thing 100 percent. Create a habit of accomplishing one thing before moving on to the next. Set your mind, your heart, and your goals on focusing and finishing. There's no problem with multi-tasking or having multiple businesses, in fact that's to be celebrated. However you should always keep in mind and ask yourself, what is my end goal and does this benefit my future plans. A few years ago I signed up to work with this multi-level marketing company, which added health and beauty products to my website. Did it fit the You're Beautiful Honie brand of health, wealth, beauty, and encouragement? Yes! Was it beneficial to my future goals and plans? Unfortunately, it wasn't. I couldn't focus on building my company and someone else's at the same time, building a team for that company instead of building a team for my company, marketing and promoting their products instead of marketing and promoting mine. In order to be successful with that company I had to rob mine; of time, energy, and resources. I had to refocus, and figure out what my end goal was.

Where in your life could you be more focused? Where could you be focusing more of your time, effort, and energy? With family to fix broken bonds, on school work to graduate, with a spouse to repair your marriage, with yourself to build confidence, or in therapy to heal past wounds? Are you sold on the end goal or are you just dancing around it?

Sickness or Poor Health
It is health that is real wealth and not pieces of gold and silver.
—Gandhi

Look at yourself and think about whether you're in the best shape possible. If not, are doing anything to change that? If you're not living a healthy lifestyle, ask yourself why. People neglect their health and fitness for many reasons. But our health is our number-one asset; without it we have nothing. Poor diet and failure to maintain weight can lead to heart disease, diabetes, hypertension, high cholesterol, infertility, back pain, skin infections, ulcers, gallstones, stress, and depression. It can increase your chances of cancer by up to 50 percent. Poor diet and obesity can also have a damaging effect on your immune system, making it difficult for your body to fight everyday illnesses. All of these diseases and ailments can have adverse effects on your lifestyle and progress. There are many foods that can alter your mood, cognitive abilities, and chemical balances. Studies have shown the correlation between foods like sugar and caffeine with depression, addiction, stress, and ADHD. In addition, being overweight often leads to poor self-esteem and self-image, causing a lack of confidence, which is vital when trying to move forward in any area of your life. If your procrastination stems from a poor diet, lack of exercise, and a limited amount of energy or mobility, I suggest that you seek professional help from someone who is trained and can help you reach your health and fitness goals.

     If you have a debilitating disease or illness that you cannot help with the change of your diet or lifestyle, that doesn't mean your life is over. If you are procrastinating because of a physical disability, find a way that works for you. I used to work for a television news show, and I have seen medical mysteries of triumph that will blow your mind. Seeing those stories always kept me humbled and gracious. Take it from me, you're not alone. With help from others, I'm sure you can achieve whatever your heart desires. I've seen people without limbs become champions and people with terrible diseases become business owners and stars. We are all subject to some level of pain and suffering in our lives. You have to make up your mind that your desire for a better life is greater than your desire to remain the same. When you put your mind to something and commit to it, things will change, regardless of your disability or physical limitations. Just try! Don't delay; you owe it to yourself. There is a support group for almost everything and everyone. Surround yourself with people who understand what you're going through, people who can help motivate you to move forward, and people who will inspire you to live your greatest life. The love of my life is one of the most prominent thought leaders when it comes to diversity and inclusion. Day in and day out I see him fight for people and groups that experience disparities of all types. He's a champion for those voices that are unheard, but you have to speak up. I promise that if you reach out, someone will be there to grab your hand. We serve, we give our lives, we dedicate our time to helping people; but we are not the only ones. There are tons of people who are looking to help those in need of a stretched hand.

    What resources do you need to seek out in order to live a healthier lifestyle? Is your ailment more physical or mental? Are you doing all you can do to strengthen yourself mentally and physically?

Final Thought
Telling someone who procrastinates to buy a weekly planner is like telling someone with chronic depression to just cheer up.
—Dr. Joseph Ferrari

Most of what we've covered thus far about procrastination can fall under the categories of low self-esteem or lack of confidence. The things we fear most about moving forward are all in our minds. Stop telling yourself the lies. There is nothing on the other side of fear or failure that will kill you. There are only lessons and experiences, both of which make you a better person. I understand that doing something different, getting out of your comfort zone, taking risks, and putting in the work isn't easy. But I promise you, it's worth it. You will be stronger, wiser, and more equipped to handle life's challenges in the end. In addition, pushing through and achieving your goals, even the small ones; create the antidote to low self-esteem by providing confidence. It helps you to build a foundation of trust in yourself for the next goal or project. Quite frankly, when I accomplish personal goals, it always brings a great sense of happiness and joy to my heart. When I achieve something great, I look back in awe at the journey. When I stop procrastinating, get down to business, and work my butt off, there's a completely overwhelming feeling of fulfillment. Why? Because I realize that I may have to bend, but I will never have to be broken to succeed. It's all in your mind, release the negative thoughts and just do what you have to do in order to obtain the life you deserve!

Practice makes perfect. So create a sense of urgency in your life today! Figure out what you need to do today to generate some activity and action in your life. What would you do differently if you only had one year left to live? If you say you're going to do something, do it. I remember watching Lisa Nichols in an interview once. She was describing a conversation she had with someone in Africa. There was an interpreter relaying her words to the person she was speaking to. They were asking her if she was going to attend an event. Over and over again, she kept replying "I will try." This went on for a few minutes until the interpreter explained to Lisa that there is no word or translation in their language for *try*. You're either going to do something or you're not. Commit to yourself and your dreams. Don't fret over the minor details and stall. Learn to live in the moment of action. Don't overwhelm yourself with fears, insecurities, and concerns so much that you abandon the task altogether. Just take the first step and show some initiative toward completing your goal. Take the risk, leap with faith, and shoot for the moon. It's okay if you fall amongst the stars.

3
Drop the Negativity
Create and maintain a more positive existence

The Fire

You've finally decided to get up, get out of the fire, and move on with your life, but somehow there's still something holding you back. You are faced with the flames. These are negative thoughts, negative people, negative environments, and negative distractions that have been ruling your world for way too long. Sometimes these flames can be really hard to fight on your own. That's why we have firefighters (true friends, family members, life coaches, mentors, therapists, and counselors). Everything the flames touch will be destroyed. They disintegrate hopes, dreams, and aspirations for a better future. These flames can be strong; I've been there. They come in forms of masked love, addiction, depression and complacency. These flames can be extremely aggressive and persistent at times, leaving you feeling weak and helpless. Just remember, you have the power to extinguish the flames by using positivity. You can and will extinguish the flames that are destroying your existence by practicing a positive lifestyle and avoiding the very sparks of the flame, which are negative thoughts and limiting beliefs you've grown accustomed to over the years. You have the ability to manifest and attract positivity in your life, and I'm going to teach you how.

Mindset Transformation

So, now that you've actually stopped procrastinating and you're ready to move on your dreams and aspirations, what comes next? Mindset transformation! It's time to clean house. It's time for you to rid your world, your life, your relationships, your health, and your mind of any negativity—anything that doesn't positively benefit your existence. Yes, you! You will be doing the cleaning, because happiness and peace is a decision you make. You have a choice to live a joyous, fulfilling, love-filled, and prosperous life. Often, it's not the world that's holding you back—it's you. Your mind isn't right. It's not your boss, it's not your coworkers, it's not your parents, it's not your family, it's not your spouse, and it's certainly not God. You have to stop blaming everyone and everything else for your problems. You, your thinking, your actions, and what you allow in your life sets the tone for your problems. The negativity and the attraction of negative people, places, and things begins in your mind with your thoughts.

Where you are right now is a direct result of the choices, actions, and decisions you've made in the past. Once you can own up to that, you can begin to move forward. You have to accept your part in where you are today, or you won't progress. You chose the job, you chose the spouse, and you choose to allow certain people to treat you a certain way. Earlier I spoke about learning how to own my problems. I chose to drop out of school, I chose to get into a relationship with a man I knew was an abusive alcoholic, and I was the one who chose to live a life of existing over living. It wasn't until I started looking in the mirror that things began to change. Once I accepted the fact that I had made all those choices, it clicked. If I made those choices, I had the capability to make new choices, to take different action, and to make better decisions moving forward. Taking hold of that power, the power of choice, was the best decision I ever made.

But I get it. Sometimes we just can't get out of the rut, accept our mistakes, and move forward because we simply feel torn down. We lack the self-confidence it takes to fight the flames. In order for progress to happen in your life, you have to believe in yourself more than anyone else does. No amount of external negativity should faze you. This section of the book will help you become more equipped to handle and extinguish the flames in your life.

Do me a favor and answer the following questions to yourself.

Do you value yourself?
Are you working a job you hate for an amount of money that doesn't represent your worth?
What does self-worth mean to you?
Are you in a healthy relationship? Is positive, encouraging, peaceful, and growing? Or is it demeaning, disrespectful, and lacking equality?
What is your attitude toward yourself like?
Do you say things to or about yourself that would make you uncomfortable if someone else said them to you?

How happy are you with the type of person you've become?
Are you proud of who you are, your character, and how you treat people?
How well do you manage challenges and stress in your life?
Do you lack strength and resilience? Do you crumble at the sight of difficulty?
Do you have a high level of confidence in your abilities overall?
When you set out to accomplish something, do you feel defeated before you even start?
Do you constantly compare yourself to others?
Do you feel inferior physically, mentally, socially, or financially?

Are you happy with your responses?

There is no quick fix or final solution when it comes to building self-worth, confidence and a life of positivity. It's a learning process that requires a lifestyle of ongoing habits and practices. It's something that you have to work at until it becomes second nature to you. There will always be new experiences and situations that test your character, your strength, your morals, and your ability to remain positive and look at the brighter side of life. It's how you respond to those negative emotions that makes all the difference in the world. To extinguish the negativity in your life, you have to be committed to utilizing these tools, dedicated to implementing new techniques, and eliminate certain habits from your life.

It really is quite simple when you finally wrap your mind around it. Some folks want you to believe that it's complicated, a secret, or something that only a certain type of individual can grasp. That's foolish. Anyone can grasp the concept of living a more positive, fulfilled life if—and only if—they want to. Not because anyone else told them to but because they truly desire it for themselves. Deep down inside they know that somehow they deserved better and that they are capable of being better. Everyone deserves to feel great about themselves, who they are, and what they do. We should all be striving toward a life of positivity, happiness, health, wealth, and prosperity. We all have the capacity to change our world. When are you going to believe it, act on it, and begin living the life you've always wanted?

What is it that you're really hoping to get out of life? Where do you want to be? What are some of your biggest concerns about where you are right now? What's holding you back? Whatever the answers are, I can almost guarantee that if you take charge of your life, implement the recommendations in this book, and dedicate the time, you will be in a totally different place next year and forevermore.

So, let's get started. Let's learn how to create a positive mental space for your confidence to live. People often feed the negative thinking that damages their self-esteem. Negative thoughts, feelings, and emotions can't successfully manifest when you develop a positive mental state. Often times, people have these feelings of self-doubt, fear, worry, self-persecution, and failure because they don't know to process their thoughts. They don't know how to categorize, eliminate, or change them. No one teaches us how to acknowledge these thoughts, address them, and simply replace them with more positive, powerful thoughts that will empower us. You have to learn how identify the situation, and begin to explore your thoughts, feelings, and emotions *before* you can begin to change them. It's called emotional intelligence. Understanding, discerning, and regulating your thoughts and emotions is key to maintaining change.

      I'm going to help you develop a stronger sense of control over your thoughts and emotions; allowing you to have a stronger sense of control over you actions. This chart will help you identify those emotions, triggers, thoughts, and actions that create your lifestyle. You might want to create a blank one for yourself on a separate sheet of paper to help guide you.

	Example
Situation	My tire blew out on the highway
Triggers	Unexpected delay, expense, and hassle
Thought	I have such bad luck—this type of stuff always happens to me
Emotion	Anger, fear, anxiety, stress
Action	Becomes flustered, yells over the phone, impatient with and rude to agent
Lifestyle	Always upset, fears the worst, pessimistic, and high strung

We don't realize that our thoughts have a significant and direct effect on our mood, emotions, and overall feelings of self-worth. It's a ripple effect. When you feed into those negative thoughts, they become emotions, and emotions become actions. Those actions become habits, and habits become a way of life. Therefore, your thoughts become your life! I'm sure you've heard that many times before, but maybe no one has ever broken it down and showed you how. Let's go over it again just for safety, and then I want you to think of a time when this has happened in your life. Your thoughts (negative or positive) transform into emotions, emotions turn into actions, actions turn into habits, and habits become your lifestyle. Take a second and let it sink in. You have the power to change your current existence. But you have to shift your thought patterns and take control of your emotions, actions, and life for that to happen. I know, I know. You're thinking this is way easier said than done, right? Well, if that's how you feel, so be it. The universe will adhere to everything you say. So, for you, maybe it will be tough. But things will begin to shift for the person who says, "I will try; I can do this!" As I said before, most of our difficulties, challenges, and barriers start in our minds. The problems in our lives, our careers, our relationships, our families, and, most importantly, within ourselves all start in our minds.

If you don't think you're good enough, you're probably not. If you don't think your marriage will work, it won't. If you don't think your child will ever succeed in life, that will always be your perception. When you entertain negative thoughts you project that energy out into the universe. The ultimate goal from now on is for you to confront those negative thoughts, acknowledging and recognizing that they do exist. Once you recognize a negative thought creeping around in your head, catch it! Grab ahold of it and whisper to yourself, "I see you, I feel you, but I will not let you control me."

What do you do once you've caught that pesky little good-for-nothing negative thought—the one that says that you can't do it, that you're ugly, that your competitor has so much more to offer than you, that life sucks, that you couldn't have a successful business even if you tried, and that love will never come your way? What do you do with that negative thought that says you should just give up? Discard it, eliminate it, and replace it with a positive thought. It may seem like you're lying to yourself at first. But it only sounds that way because you, your parents, your teachers, your spouse, your friends, and your family have been lying to you for so many years, brainwashing you into believing some of those negative thoughts about yourself. If someone tells you that you're fat, dumb, and ugly enough times, at some point you're going to believe that you're fat, dumb, and ugly. We all believed in Santa Claus, the Easter Bunny, and the Tooth Fairy at some point. It's time for you to create a new wave of thinking with positive thoughts that will motivate, empower, and inspire you to be a different person. It's all about reprogramming your mind and not allowing other people's fears and insecurities take up space in your head. At first it may feel awkward, but fake it until you make it. Just keep exercising your mind until it grows strong enough to fight those negative thoughts. This is definitely a process. It all depends on how damaged your thinking is and how long you've been fed the lies that have put limitations on your life. But again, if you do the work, you will not be disappointed.

We'll start with some introductory mindfulness using gratitude, mantras, and affirmations.

Gratitude

One of the easiest ways for you to move forward in positive thinking is by practicing gratitude. There's a song by Hezekiah Walker called "Grateful," and every time I'm in church and the choir starts singing this song, I start bawling. Tears flow down my face and I can't hold it in—yes, it's the big ol' ugly nobody-look-at-me cry. Why? Because I begin to think of all the ways I am blessed. I start running down a list in my head and begin to feel the genuine gratitude in my heart for all that I have in this world. I begin to think of all the things I've been through and my journey toward healing myself and others. I begin to feel foolish about complaining about the insignificant and meaningless things in life. I begin praising and worshiping God for all the things I do have. I praise and worship him for my life, home, food, the safety of my family, and for all the love I have in my life. When you stop focusing on what you don't have, what's wrong, and all the negative things in your life and start focusing on what you do have, what is right, and all the positive things in your life, your mentality and your life will change. Getting to that positive state of being is much easier with gratitude.

As discussed, life is full of uncertainties and disappointments, that's the reality of being here and alive on earth. The beauty of this is that no matter who we are or what our situation looks like, we all have more than enough to be thankful for. Gratitude and appreciation have a way of easing and healing our pain. Taking time out of each day to appreciate all the blessings you have can be the difference between having a good day and having a great one. We wake up each day with a choice in how we are going to move forward. It's not by the week or by the year, but by the day. None of us are promised the next hour or minute. So if you have breath in your body the choice to be grateful should be an easy one.

When you wake up, remember you have a choice to be grateful; no matter what your current situation is. I always say that while everyone else is arguing over whether the glass is half-full or half-empty, I'm just happy to have a glass and that there's something in it. We have the ability to choose happiness in all scenarios. You have to learn how to see the possibilities in your problems and the options in your obstacles. It's all about perception. Who taught you that the glass was half-empty—your parents, your teacher, your spouse? When do you start feeling good about what's actually in your glass? When it's filled to the brim? There are individuals whose cup runneth over, and they are still unhappy. It's not about the cup or what's in it—it's about you and being happy with what's inside of you.

How often do you really stop and think about how blessed you are as opposed to focusing on how unfortunate you are? How often do you acknowledge the great things in your life that you are happy about? How often do you thank God for your family, friends, support system, place to stay, food to eat, clothes on your back, safety, and simply being alive? How often do you reflect on the fact that things could be a lot worse for you and that your life really isn't as bad as you make it out to be? How often are you truly thankful for what you already have? How often do you reflect on how strong you are, and how you made it through? Because if you're reading this, you still haven't given up, which is a great thing! But how can the universe bless you with a more abundant life if you don't appreciate the one you already have?

You should remind yourself every day of all the fortune you possess, and you should take a second to think of those who don't have any of the things you do. Say a quick prayer for those who are less fortunate, and reflect on what your life would be like if you didn't have some of the luxuries that you are most thankful for. When you wake up in the morning, before you go to bed, or all throughout the day, you should be reflecting on all the reasons why you are grateful. This should be a part of your daily routine. When you truly realize how blessed you are, the little things won't bother you. You won't harbor such negative, depressing, downtrodden thoughts and feelings about your life. When you escape those feelings and start experiencing the joyous feelings of gratefulness, you will open your life up to receiving more positivity and more abundance. I believe that having an "attitude of gratitude," as they say, is one of the first steps to happiness and to opening the door to a whole new life.

Take a second to reflect. I want you to fill out these blank lines accordingly. Try to truly feel the emotion of gratitude for these things. Feel free to add or create your own gratitude list on a separate sheet of paper.

What are you thankful for?
I am grateful for my basic necessities.
    1. _____
    2. _____
    3. _____
I am grateful for my family.
    1. _____
    2. _____
    3. _____
I am grateful for my friends.
    1. _____
    2. _____
    3. _____
I am grateful for…
    1. _____
    2. _____
    3. _____

Here are a few ways you can use your gratitude list:
1. When you wake up, reflect on this sheet so that you can start your day off with a pleasant feeling of already having more than enough to be thankful for.
2. Before you go to bed, reflect on one good thing that happened during the day. Write it down on your gratitude sheet and expect something good to happen the next day as well!

3. When you encounter a challenge, remember your past wins and how strong and triumphant you were. Understand that this difficult situation won't last forever. Be reminded that there's always someone who would jump to be in your shoes. Learn from the situation, and be grateful that growth, wisdom, strength, and preparation for the future come with experience.

Mantras & Affirmations

The second thing that really helped me get into a positive mind-set was living by a mantra and using positive affirmations. The two are different yet very similar. A mantra should represent your overarching beliefs. This word or saying should bring you to a place of focus and calm. A mantra is often used during meditation, yoga, or in situations where you are experiencing high anxiety. Affirmations are phrases, repeated daily, that support your mantra.

Let's first explore the mantra. Again, it's a statement that is repeated frequently, often to reestablish a centering thought or feeling. It's commonly used in meditation to bring forth a level of concentration. I use mantras to generate peace within myself. I also use them as part of my moral and spiritual compass to overcome certain character flaws. They are phrases that I live by; a true way of life.

If you are impatient, and you find yourself saying things to yourself like: "Ugh, I don't have time for this. I hate waiting. I will never get there on time." What if you replaced those thoughts with a positive mantra such as, "Patience is a virtue; I am a man/woman of peace." So when you're waiting in line at the grocery store and feel yourself becoming anxious or annoyed, grab ahold of that negative thought or feeling, take control of it, replace it with your mantra, and allow yourself to come back to a place of peace and centeredness. Be aware and in control of the moment. You have the power to change your mood, attitude, and actions at any given moment. Take pride in that power! Use your mantras to help you create the person you want to be.

    Your character often precedes you in many ways. Who you are and how you make people feel is significant when you're striving for a life of love, success, health, wealth, and happiness. Do you think people want to be around someone who is always complaining? Do you think professionals want to associate themselves with people who are naysayers and can't control their negative emotions? Do you think people enjoy being surrounded by people who have low self-esteem? Do you inspire people? Do you encourage their spirits? Your way of life, how you move, what comes out your mouth, and how you respond to people clearly shows your way of thinking. You should develop mantras that represent the type of life you want to lead.

Here are some popular mantras you can start with:
- I am whole, strong, powerful, loving, harmonious, and happy.
- I stay connected to and am guided by my inner source.
- I am a magnet for joy, love, and abundance.
- The past has no power over the present.
- There are no failures—just experiences and my reactions to them.
- If I change my thoughts, I can change my world.
- Change is growth. I will seek new environments, new people, and new experiences.
- Health is wealth. I will respect my body because it is a temple.
- I am an attractive being. The light within me shines.
- I am wealthy in all that I do. God is my supplier.

I encourage you to do more research on mantras in general and find out how you can use them in your life to better your overall experience.

Now let's talk about affirmations. Affirmations are to be used every day. Yep, that's right. Each and every day, I repeat affirmations to myself over and over again. Affirmations are carefully formatted statements that should be written down and repeated to yourself daily. I use Post-It to help me remain consistent. I have them posted all over the wall in front of my computer in my office. Daily affirmations are a huge part of exercising your mind. The goal is to retrain your thinking, so you must do it on a daily basis, until it becomes second nature.

  You don't have to use Post-It notes like I do. Be creative! Print some of your affirmations on colorful paper, cut them out, and put them on a vision board. If you are an artist, paint something that inspires or triggers a positive thought for you. Put your affirmation on a canvas and frame it, hang it up in your home. This way, you are constantly surrounded by positivity and inspiration. Put an affirmation alarm on your phone. Every time your phone alerts you, you can repeat the affirmation to yourself. Get a small journal—one you can carry with you or keep in your car—and write your affirmations down over and over again. I particularly love journals. Every day I write in my journal —affirmations, prayers, gratitude lists, things I envision for my future, and anything positive, uplifting, or inspiring.

  If you enjoy writing, try the five-year-letter assignment. You can do this by writing a letter to a friend (yourself) dated five years from today. In this letter, you should write as though all your goals and dreams have come true. Write it as though all your affirmations about success, happiness, love, prosperity, health, and freedom have manifested. Take the letter and put it somewhere safe so you can open it up in five years and see how far you've come. Affirm, affirm, affirm greatness in your life.

The key is to engulf yourself in positivity. When you begin to change your outlook on life, when you stop procrastinating and begin following your dreams, and when you decide to change, you will be faced with a lot of negativity—so important that you be prepared. Affirmations will help you build the confidence you need to move towards positivity and optimism. However it's important that you create good ones. When you speak your affirmations, you should feel them deep in your spirit; they shouldn't feel like a chore. Each affirmation should provide you with great inspiration, motivation, and confidence. It should be tailored to your life and your current situation. My affirmations may not work for you and vice versa. You have to dig deep and see where you need the most transformation. Then create affirmations that will spark change in those areas.

Here are a couple of tips for creating great affirmations:
1. Your affirmations should be written and spoken in the present tense. (For example, "I am sufficient. My knowledge, wisdom, and experience are more than enough to help someone else in their struggle.")
2. Your affirmations should be repeated daily. Use Post-Its, symbols, alarms, and vision boards to remind you.
3. Your affirmations should be meaningful. They should be things that you truly desire for yourself—things that will have

a true impact on your life. Thus, when you say them, you feel them.

Here are some examples:
- I am strong enough to handle whatever comes my way.
- I am a great mother/father, wife/husband, sister/brother.
- I am proud of the person I've become.
- I am worthy of greatness.
- I am thankful for my life; I am blessed in all I do.
- My influence is positive and powerful.
- My life has a purpose.
- I deserve love, kindness, and respect.
- I can and will achieve whatever I set my mind to.
- This is my time to shine and I will not dim my light for anyone!

It may feel weird in the beginning, because you may not be living up to your own expectations. You may not feel like you're a good spouse or think you can handle stress, but don't worry. The right affirmations will provide you with a sense of accountability. If you wake up and say throughout the day that you are a positive person who spreads light and love, you will think twice cursing someone out. And with this practice you will slowly but surely see change.

The mantras and affirmations are like tools for cleansing the soul, for getting rid of all that doubt and negative self-talk. I guarantee you that when you pair a strong mantra with powerful affirmations; you will be on your way to achieving great success in all areas of your life. People will gravitate toward you and will want to help you succeed. I enjoy working with and surrounding myself with strong, positive people who are confident about their abilities.

Mindset Transformation Exercise
1. You've learned how to identify your negative thoughts so you can begin to shift your mindset.
2. You've learned how to highlight what you're grateful for in effort to live a more grateful life.
3. You've learned how to retrain your brain to think more positively and create a more positive existence by using mantras and affirmations.

Now, let's transform your thinking by using all three of these techniques together. I will be using the same example from pg. 53 if you'd like to refer back to it.

Negative Thought
"Oh my God! I can't believe I got a blowout on the highway. I'm so upset. I can't believe this is happening to me. I have such bad luck. I'm so upset and angry right now. I'm going to be so late. What am I going to do?"
You can continue to complain about it throughout the day, spreading the negativity to other people, living in the negativity for days by repeating the story over and over again. Or you can move on to your grateful thought.

Grateful Thought
"Thank God I didn't cause an accident. I'm glad no one was severely injured. I am so lucky that the traffic was light and that I could get over to the shoulder. I am grateful that someone stopped to help me."
Grab ahold of that feeling of gratitude, and really reflect for a second to calm yourself down. Use your mantra to bring you back to a place of centeredness.

Affirmation
"I'm glad it's still light out and I have a cell phone. I can let my loved ones know that I'm safe. I am blessed to have the resources to get a new tire. I truly appreciate the person who stopped to help me. I'm glad I could make it to the repair shop before they closed."
Follow up with an affirmation: "I can handle any challenge that comes my way. I never become a victim to my circumstances."

4
Drop Negative People

Have you ever heard of the saying, "Elevation requires separation?" I know and understand that at this point in my book people will become extremely uncomfortable. Some people will simply find this task too daunting, as it requires them to go against their own emotions, desires, and people that they love. But separating yourself from those who bring negativity into your world is a must. I understand it's hard, but I can guarantee you that as long as you allow these people to remain in your life, and treat you the way they do, your growth and progress will be stifled by them. The flames will continue to ravage through your life.

Sometimes we love too hard, and end up giving people the power over our emotions and well-being. But it doesn't have to be that way. You can love someone, have a great deal of respect for them, and treat them well without letting them take advantage of you or bring negativity into your world. Some people know that if they're high on someone's list of importance, they can get away with murder. Don't let that be the case with you! You deserve respect, honor, and love just like everyone elsc in this world.

You should be surrounding yourself with people who love you, encourage you, support you, and make you happy. Take a second and think about what your life would be like if all the negative, hurtful, and disrespectful people disappeared or changed? You have to take control of your circle and realize that you can choose the individuals with whom you associate. Jim Rohn says that, "We are the average of the five people we spend the most time with." What does that say about you? If you are always in trouble, in financial ruin, unable to land a job, sick, overweight, unable to build a strong and lasting romantic relationship, or simply unhappy, take a look at the people around you and ask yourself if those people are influencing your life. If they are, make it a point to change your circle accordingly, you'll begin to see an entirely new shift in your world.

There's at least one person on your mind right now you're thinking you're life would be better without. But your mind is going: I just can't get away from them; we're too close. I love them. There is no way that I can eliminate them from my life. They need me. I need them! What will I do without them? It's just not possible. Well, for one thing, quit with the negative self-talk. Whatever you say you can't do, you most certainly won't do. You are the star of your own show in this thing called life, right? Right! Let's say your life is on the main stage, right? Right! In the theater, there are only a certain number of available seats in the front row, right? Right! Take a second and think about who deserves to be in that front row? These seats should be held for those people who love you, encourage you, respect you, and make you happy. Some people need to be sitting in the orchestra, while others may need to be seated in the mezzanine. There are a few people in your life who need to be seated a bit farther away, like up in the balcony seats. Then, there are a few people who need to be escorted out of the theater altogether.

Keep in mind as we move forward in this chapter that I'm not referring to those who love you and bring positivity and joy to your world. It's up to you to discern who is causing disruption, negativity, and pain in your life and adjust their access to you accordingly. You have to challenge yourself to make the appropriate decisions about negative people in your life.

Now let's get to it
Parents

You can't change your parents. I'm not saying that you literally "drop" your parent/s. But as with everyone in this chapter, you should establish boundaries where necessary. If you don't have difficult parents, perfect! More power to you. When I discuss parents in this chapter, I am referring to those who have parents that played or play a major part in holding them back or causing severe emotional distress. I'm talking to those who have an extremely tumultuous relationship with their parents; those who have been abused, abandoned, and been through tragedy with their parents.

Having a disagreement with your parents doesn't mean that they are bad. Everyone has disagreements. For example, we live in an age in which evolution seems to be happening in triple time and technology is moving at the speed of light. It can be hard for parents to keep up and understand why and how some things have changed so drastically. My parents and grandparents lived in a time when they could get a factory or corporate job, work for forty years, have a great pension, and retire happily. That isn't necessarily the case today. If you're not a doctor, lawyer, an engineer, or in technology, you'd better be extremely creative, innovative, and in tune with your skills and abilities. Technology has eliminated so many careers, and computers have revolutionized how we do everything. This has become the age of entrepreneurship. Everyone's becoming his or her own boss. Some parents may not understand how you're making money on Instagram or Facebook. They may not agree with you quitting your day job to follow your dreams. They may think it's risky and discourage you. This example is typical. You don't need "boundaries" for typical family disagreements.

    Now, if your parents are constantly telling you what you can't do, how you are wrong, and why you'll never amount to anything if you don't follow this route or take that path—that's not productive or healthy. Sometimes parents are scared, afraid, and they project their fears and insecurities on you. I remember my mom didn't want me to play basketball, thinking I might get hurt. Years later I played softball and proved to be a great athlete. Then I wanted to gain some experience modeling, but her worry was that someone would take advantage of me and hurt me. I ended up disregarding a letter I received from the Miss New Jersey USA pageant because of her wishes. When I was a senior in high school, I received a full scholarship to Texas Southern

University. My mother thought it was "too far," that if something happened, it would be difficult for her to get there. She planted so many seeds of fear in me. However, those were *her* fears, *her* anxieties, and *her* worries. They weren't mine. As we become adults, we have to learn how to separate our fears from those of our parents.

I've seen people choose careers they hated because their parents encouraged them to. I've seen people live every day in misery, questioning their own abilities because they never followed their dreams. I've seen people get married to people they weren't in love with and have children when they weren't ready because of the pressure from their parents. I've seen women stay in unhealthy relationships because their parents taught them that security and being taken care of was the most important thing in a relationship. I've seen men stay at home well into their forties with no partner, no children, and no life because they've become the man in their mother's life. Let's face it—some of us have put our happiness in the hands of our parents'.

I used to allow my mother to hold my happiness hostage. I've always been an honor student. I got accepted into one of the best high schools in the region, graduated with honors from Kean University, and obtained a competitive internship at CBS. I remained on staff with one of the highest-rated shows in the country, I started my own women's empowerment company, founded a nonprofit, received countless awards and accolades, and successfully completed an accelerated master's program. Yet all I ever wanted was for my mother to say, "I'm proud of you." I work twice as hard, thinking that one day my life's work will fix our relationship. I thought if I showed her how great I was, she would accept me for the woman I've grown to be. The truth is that I may never get that. I've always wanted validation from my mother, but she has thoughts, ideas, and beliefs about me that I can't change. Am I supposed to rest my confidence and happiness in her hands? Absolutely not, and you shouldn't rest yours in the hands of your parents either. You can't change how your parents view your life. If you're waiting for them to accept your career, your spouse, your children, or your lifestyle in order to be happy, you may never be happy. Is that a chance you're willing to take?

Through counseling, growth, and wisdom, I've learned how to meet people where they are. We have to love our parents for exactly who they are, not who we expect them to be. The moment I let go, the moment I stopped wishing my mother would do this or do that, the moment I accepted who she was, things changed. I stopped feeding the disagreements, stopped allowing her words to cut me so deeply, and I stopped anticipating the negativity. When I stopped expecting her to be someone she wasn't, we began to make incredible headway. Things shifted once I created boundaries and accepted our relationship for what it was. We've made tremendous progress learning and accepting one another. It's not perfect but it's much better. We can truly hear each other clear now that we have boundaries with one another.

If you feel like the relationship you have with your parents causes you to be under a tremendous amount of emotional distress, it's okay to create boundaries. We should have boundaries with everyone in our lives. You have the right to step back, build up your self-esteem, and demand love and respect. Being a parent doesn't give someone an "I can hurt you and get away with it" pass. Be strong in who you are, who you want to be, how you want to live, who you want to marry, and your personal life decisions. Those major life decisions and choices are yours. This is no practice run. This is real life; you don't get a do-over. When you look back, you want to be sure that you lived for you, not just for your parents. You don't want to look back and realize that none of the decisions you made were for you and your happiness. When people truly love you, they want to see you happy. Work towards healing but don't allow the journey to break you down. Don't give someone else the power to control your emotions.

Family

I've seen so many scenarios with complicated dynamics in which people need to need to create and enforce boundaries with their family members. We do not get to choose who we are related to—period. We can't undo our bloodlines. The family we have is the family we got, and that's that—nothing more and nothing less. The unfortunate thing about family is that we often give them a free pass to hurt us because they are family. We give them chance after chance after chance, hoping that things will change, because we are trained to believe that's what family is supposed to do. So, are we all just expected to roll over and take the crap because our DNA matches? Should we let people disrespect us, hurt us, and take advantage of us because we're related? Should we accept individuals that act foolish at our most important functions, commit heinous crimes against us, drive us crazy, and rob us of so much just because they're family? When will enough be enough or you? When will you stand up for yourself and let those family members know that you will not tolerate anything less than what you deserve?

Spouse

If your stomach just turned, if your heart skipped a beat, if you just became anxious, or if you can't wait to see what I'm about to say about leaving your spouse, you've probably already thought about it, someone has suggested it to you, or maybe something needs to change in your relationship for there to be peace. Everyone has different standards of what love looks like. We establish our first idea of love and how to show it from the time we're infants until we're about five. That's our foundation for everything we know about love. Our parents were our first examples of how to love. Did you grow up with both your parents? Were they married? Did they hug and kiss? Did they shower each other with love? Did they shower you with love? What did that love look like? Did they celebrate each other's accomplishments and support each other's dreams? Did they always speak in a respectful tone and manner? Did you see them fighting often? Was there infidelity? Was there abuse or drug use? Did they divorce? If so was it an amicable split? The answers to these questions have a big impact on how you view love, what you will tolerate in a relationship, and the many dynamics that take place between you and your partner.

There are many different ways to tell whether it's time to leave your partner. The most important reasons to leave are for the sake of your mental, spiritual, emotional, and physical health. Abuse in any of these areas should not be tolerated on any level. Love is not enough, and it should not be used as an excuse to stay in an abusive relationship. When people hear the term abuse, they often think of physical abuse. There are so many other ways a person can abuse you. It's just often disguised by apologies, lies, promises, gifts, trips, sex, guilt, and a host of other things that will keep you blind to what's really going on. Just because someone isn't physically putting his or her hands on you doesn't mean you aren't suffering from some type of mental, spiritual, or emotional abuse. If you are in a situation that is causing constant hurt, disappointment, pain, anger, or any other negative emotion or distress, you should be taking a step back to evaluate why you are allowing this type of negativity in your life, especially from someone who is supposed to be there to create a positive, safe environment for you to flourish in the relationship.

Are you in a relationship that lacks consideration, respect, compromise, communication, support, encouragement, fun, and simply a place to retreat when the world gets tough? You can have a strong love for someone, truly care about the person, and share total affection with him or her, and still not have a healthy relationship. Marriage can't be solely based on the fact that you love a person. Are you compatible? Do you have the same vision or aspirations for your life together? Do your future goals align? Is your partner understanding, accepting, and supportive of your goals and dreams? Does he or she have the same values and morals as you? Do you agree on the important things in life? Like, how to discipline your children or what religion you will raise them in? All of these things matter when you're in a long-term relationship and potentially growing a family. You can love someone and yet disagree on every one of those topics. Would that make for a happy, healthy relationship?

     So often, people jump into relationships, and they don't have a thing in common with their partner. Technology and social media have altered our sense of reality. Dating is completely different today. You have to find a way to break through the facade and get to the core of a person, before you marry them and have children. So many people get married for the wrong reasons (money, looks, kids, security, social status, etc), and then they are miserable or end up going outside the relationship to find what they need. The marriage may last for a little while, but eventually, if you don't genuinely enjoy your partner, it will fall apart. If you are unhappy because you and your spouse are on two different levels, unequally yoked, and your differences are becoming more and more visible as time goes on, then you need to ask yourself, "How long am I willing to remain in a relationship in which I'm not fulfilled or happy?"

I'm not saying that you should just give up and walk away. There are two types of conflicts: solvable problems and irreconcilable differences. That's why I always suggest that when you are dating, you should know what your "negotiables" and "non-negotiables" are. If you accept a non-negotiable in the dating phase, it may come back to bite you as an irreconcilable problem in the long run. You have to make better decisions going into the relationship, because it's much more difficult to let go when you've begun a long-term relationship with someone. If the problem is solvable then (the both of you) work at it and try to fix it. Both of you have to make the effort toward change. If it's an irreconcilable difference that's creating a miserable existence for you, then you may want to look at your options. I'm not here to promote breakups or divorce, which is why I suggest doing the work prior to getting serious. I do, however, promote mental, emotional, spiritual, and physical health. And unfortunately, sometimes it's a romantic relationship that is causing the deterioration of one or all of those major life pillars.

I have been in mentally, emotionally, and physically abusive relationships and it's not fun. Nothing about them screams love. I had to learn the hard way. My mother and father were never married and separated when I was young. I never saw my mother in a serious long-term relationship. She dated a few men, but none of them became long-term partners. I never saw what a happy, healthy relationship looked like in my home. My mom never talked to me about love, standards, or what to expect from a man, and my father wasn't present. Everything I knew about relationships I learned from external influences. Keep in mind that I grew up in one of the worst cities in the country, so there wasn't exactly a host of stellar married couples to learn from. There were very few. It wasn't until I graduated college that I set my focus on self-growth, what I was worth, what was required of me in a relationship, and what I needed from a man in a relationship. I had to dig deep to find my self-worth, and I challenge anyone who's unhappy (single or in a relationship) to start there. If you're not happy in a relationship, sometimes you have to also take a look in the mirror.

     That's where it all begins. What are you worth? What do you feel like you deserve? How should you be treated in a relationship? How do you treat yourself? What do you bring to the relationship? What are you looking for in a relationship? Once you figure that out, the rest is quite simple. You either stay and accept what you feel you deserve, or you leave and find someone who will give you what you know you deserve. Deep down in our hearts, we know right from wrong. We know when we're in unhealthy relationships, when we're being held back, when we're being abused, and when we're miserable. It's all about whether you have the confidence, will, and strength to leave.

How much is your happiness worth? Your sanity? Your health? Remember, the clock is ticking and our days, numbered. How do you want to live out those days? You should be in a relationship with someone you absolutely love and adore—someone who treats you with kindness and appreciation, who will believe in you even when you can't seem to believe in yourself. You should be with someone who will push you and encourage you to follow your dreams. You should be with someone who will go out of his or her way to make you happy. You should spend those days with someone who makes you feel good about yourself. Don't forget, relationships are cyclical. You should be putting the same amount of energy, effort, and love into the relationship that you would want your partner to.

Friends and Associates

Listen, you have to be extremely cautious of the people you allow in your life. You share energy with them. Their influence will have a direct impact on your life. As children, you don't necessarily get to choose your friends. You have a few options: the kids at school, your neighbors, and the kids who participate in the same extracurricular activities as you. As you get older and go off to college or choose a career, your options open up a bit. When you hit full-on adulthood, the choice is completely up to you. That's right, it's up to you to make smart decisions about who you will and won't allow in your life. I read this saying once that said, "There are two types of people in life: assets and liabilities." That is such a raw and powerful statement, but when I thought about it, I realized how true it was. It made me rethink the way I looked at the people in my life. It may sound like a harsh statement on the surface, but it's not when you begin to realize the importance of your time and experiences here on earth. This is especially true when you begin to connect and align spiritually. Someone with an unfavorable spirit can truly become a liability in your spiritual world.

As you try to get out of the fire, there will be some people who just can't seem to be happy for you. They will be determined to tell you all the reasons why you won't be successful. They will become upset that you are spending too much time reconstructing your life and not spending enough time socializing with them. You will have some friends who will scream to save you from the fire as loud as they possibly can so that everyone can hear them while they're pouring gasoline on your front porch. You may even find out that you have some friends that lit the match. Everyone you think is your friend is not necessarily your friend. Learn how to use your discernment and use that term lightly.

The unfortunate truth is that if you really want to get out of the fire, change your life, and move forward, not everyone can go with you. Don't get me wrong—you may have absolutely amazing, incredible, loyal friends who will always be there for you. But make sure you know who they are. Acknowledge them, and keep them close. The ones who aren't genuine, the ones who tell you it's impossible, and the ones who encourage behavior that's not conducive to your success have to go. As you begin to turn your life around, not everyone will be happy or able to cope with the changes you are making in your life. People actually start to get jealous and funky when you begin to find happiness and success. It's crazy, I know, but it's true! Just remember, it's their insecurities and problems, not yours. Don't begin to blame yourself for the crumbling friendship, because they can't deal with your growth and/or success.

Think about it. What will happen to them if you change and they don't? Where will they fit in your life? Will you still associate with them? Will you just leave them behind? What if they decide they don't want to change? All these questions and so many more will be going through their mind. Abandonment is a tough feeling for people to deal with. Unfortunately, when you begin to take this journey, you won't be able to please everyone, and you won't be able to take everyone with you. How many times have we seen careers ruined in the lives of celebrities because they couldn't detach from their old life? We've seen sports figures lose it all because they couldn't separate themselves from their old friends and their shenanigans. You have to keep in mind *why* you're changing and stay focused on the end result.

Sometimes we try to create common ground where there is none, and place people we don't even like on pedestals because of social status or their connections. Too often, we give out free passes for friendship. People should have to earn your friendship, your trust, and your loyalty. Just because someone is your coworker, your neighbor, or the parent of your kid's classmate doesn't mean you're friends. You set the standard for what friendship looks like in your life and at what level. Sometimes we think people are our friends, but they are actually hurting, hindering, and enabling us. There are only two categories of people in our lives: negative or positive; there is no in-between. When your house is on fire, when you are fed up with life, when you are at your wits' end, when you are looking for healing, when you desire change, when you are ready to chase your dreams, do you want more fire fighters (positive people) or more flames (negative people)?

Let's look at a couple of examples that identify how a friendship could impact someone's life.

Example 1
Tom is looking for healing, a change; he's ready to get out of the fire and move on with his life
Jason is a friend with a negative influence
Sam is a friend with a positive influence

Scenario
Tom is trying to quit drinking. He has always been a social drinker, but last year when his cousin died, his drinking became excessive. Tom and his cousin were like brothers. Now, every time Tom drinks, he becomes irate, overwhelmed with emotion, and abusive toward his family. Tom,

Jason, and Sam are longtime friends; they met in college. They go on a fun-filled vacation every year and vow to always support each other. Both Jason and Sam are aware of Tom's heavy drinking, but they don't know about the blowups at home.

    <u>Negative Influence</u>: Jason knows that Tom is struggling with the death of his cousin. He continues to invite Tom out to the bar after work to "take a load off," expressing, Tom just needs to relax. Jason brings Tom a bottle of aged tequila as a gift when he returns from a trip to Mexico with his wife. Jason becomes upset with Tom when Tom begins to decline invitations to go out to the bar. He begins to feel like Tom doesn't enjoy his company any longer, so his attitude toward Tom begins to change. He stops checking on Tom and abandons the friendship.

    <u>Positive Influence</u>: Sam supports and respects Tom's efforts to remain sober, understanding that substance abuse can lead to serious and fatal consequences. Sam helps Tom find alternative ways of coping. He also suggests activities that don't involve alcohol. Sam allows Tom to express himself without judgment but discourages behaviors that aren't conducive to his healing. Sam sticks by Tom's side.

    Recap: Tom doesn't have to stop being Jason's friend altogether, but he may want to distance himself for a while until he gets his drinking under control. Tom has to accept that Jason just may not understand or empathize with him, and that the loss of the friendship may not mean as much to Jason. These are tough life decisions you may have to make when you are in a place of growth or healing. It will be difficult but your real friends will stick around.

Example 2
Tammy wants more out of life. She is looking for new opportunities and trying to grow.
Casey is a friend with a negative influence.
Diane is a friend with a positive influence

Scenario
Tammy is recently widowed. Her husband died in a car accident. Tammy is moving forward in her healing and wants to go back to school, so she can get a better job and move into a better neighborhood where her children can get a better education. She has a decent job now, but she'd like to begin a career in which she can save and plan for her family's future. Her husband made twice as much as she did, but they didn't have much savings. She has just about used the last of the insurance policy money to pay bills and tuition. She starts taking night classes and finds a great internship with long-term possibilities.

<u>Negative Influence</u>: Instead of being encouraging and supportive, Casey fills Tammy's head with doubt. Casey tells her she's too old to have an internship from which she receives only a stipend. She constantly reminds Tammy of the burden she's putting on her family and friends as they help out with the children while she's in school. Casey continues to paint a negative picture

for Tammy so that she loses her excitement for the future. She talks about the lack of jobs, the economy, and how people with doctorates are still on unemployment. She constantly encourages Tammy to start dating again, so that she can find someone who will take care of her like her late husband did.

<u>Positive Influence</u>: Diane doesn't mind having the kids over while Tammy's in class, and she genuinely wants to support Tammy's effort to finish school. She reminds Tammy of the advantages and possibilities of having an inside perspective as an intern. She encourages her to network and put her best foot forward. Instead of focusing on the downside of things, Diane acknowledges how far Tammy has come and reiterates that she can handle anything that comes her way. Diane prays with her and lifts her up through the hard times.

Recap: Tammy may want to rethink having Casey in her life. Casey is not only a negative influence but also has a negative mindset. Have you ever met someone who's always complaining? Nothing is ever good in their eyes. If you say it's up, they say it's down. Sometimes those people need to be eliminated from your life altogether.

Real friends should lift you up in your time of need, but some genuinely don't have that ability and don't know how to lift you up. They just aren't in the same mental space as you. That's okay, and there's nothing wrong with that, but you need to be able to recognize the divide and be ready to separate yourself appropriately if necessary. People will say that you've changed or that you're acting differently. Some people just aren't going to like the new you. Your light will be so bright that it blinds them, but you need to find a way to be okay with that. You need to be at ease with the fact that you're growing.

    Your parents, your family, your spouse, and your friends are going to say "you've changed" and when they do I encourage you to come back to this section of the book. You goal *was* to change! We don't shift every aspect of our lives to remain the same. I encourage you to keep your vision board hanging up somewhere you can see it daily, so you can remember all the reasons why you want to change! I encourage you to pay close attention to this next section and take mental notes as I take you on a journey of the extraordinary transformation of the beautiful butterfly. Hopefully it will inspire you to *keep* changing!

The Caterpillar Stage
    All a caterpillar does is eat leaves and flowers constantly—that's all it really knows how to do. This may be you right now, taking in all the knowledge. You're reading, listening, searching for a change, and trying to figure out what's the best plan of action. At this stage, because of its shape and body functions, the caterpillar is very limited in where it can go and how it can move. This is how I felt when I was growing up in Camden. I just didn't see many options. I didn't see anyone doing extraordinary things. Maybe you're at a job where

you feel limited, you do the same thing every day, and there's no excitement or fulfillment. Maybe you're in a marriage, and it's stale; there's no growth and the love has faded. Deep down inside, you know there's more out there and you know that you deserve better. Caterpillars move extremely slowly, because they have to drag their entire body. Maybe you are dragging friends, family, the past, hurt, pain, discouragement, and disappointment along with you. This is the caterpillar stage! You want to make a change, are seeking knowledge, and are maybe even trying to move, but it's not really happening yet. You're dragging too much along to make progress, and you're fearful of letting people, places, and things go.

The Molting Stage

The molting stage is when the caterpillar sheds its old shell to make room for new growth. Some animals routinely cast off parts of their bodies to make way for new growth. They may do this at different and specific points in their life cycle for their health, which means they may have to do it more than once! Shedding is routine for their health and it should be a routine for you too. Every now and again you should be evaluating where you are and who the key influencers are in your life. These key influencers may change as you grow in various stages of your life—high school, college, the beginning of your career, marriage, parenthood, and retirement. During all these phases, different people will impact your life in different ways. It's imperative that you are examining your inner circle every so often to make sure you have positive influencers who can continue to support you and help you grow.

I want to put an emphasis on the function of casting off. As I said earlier, when molting or shedding, the insect may cast off a part of its body. There are two parts to this concept. The first part is being able to let go without hope for a return. To cast off means to "throw down, let go of, discard, or let loose." Do you have a person in your life that you need to let go of without the hope for return? I'm sure we all do. We ponder, go back and forth, make excuses, and justify why we keep these people in our lives. I get it, I've been there. This is one of the most difficult things to do when you're trying to get out of the fire. But if you don't let go; cast off the negativity, the distractions, the pain, and the people who aren't serving your life in a positive way, it will all come crashing down on you. Don't be afraid to let go of the people who are holding you back from greatness or your growth.

The second part of this concept is being able to sever ties with someone you feel like is a part of you. Letting go of an abusive partner, without hope for return is one thing. Letting go of a best friend or family member; or someone who is a permanent fixture in your life is different. When animals molt, they may not just shed an outer layer of skin. In order to get ready for the next phase of their lives, they may cast off a body part. They may lose a wing that helped them fly or fur that kept them warm. They have to get rid of the old in order to make room for the new—stronger wings, a heavier coat, and bigger organs. I know what it's like to be inseparable with someone, but I also know what it's like to have to let them go. People come into your life for a reason, season, and very few stay for a lifetime. It's up to you to maintain a keen sense of awareness; understanding when to let go of those people who should only be in your life for a reason or a season.

The Pupa, or Transition, Stage

During the pupa, or transition, stage, the pupa is protected by a cocoon of silk for many months. This transition stage inside the cocoon is dark and results in a time of solitude. When I'm in a state of transition, I limit my interaction with the world. I dedicate an allotted amount of time to achieve whatever my goals are, and I focus on me and those goals. When I'm going through a transition phase "going dark" I only do and participate in things that are conducive to my health and success. I fall back from things like social media and networking or social gatherings. This becomes a time of total commitment for me. I become hyper-focused when it's time for me to stretch my goals, grow my business, continue my education, heal from a setback, or simply get aligned spiritually. I surround myself with those who believe in my dreams, inspire me, hold me accountable for my action and are geared up for success themselves.

People will say, "Girl, where have you been? You just fell off." No, I was actually hard at work. During the pupa or transition phase the cells of the larva are growing rapidly, new legs and new wings. Many of the cells are providing energy for the adult butterfly to come. So I always say, "I'm just getting charged up!" But the transition, or darkness can be tough. There are times when I'm not 100 percent, when I am struggling, trying to figure it all out. I don't know everything; I'm always learning on this journey. Life can be difficult, but it's important, even in your darkest hour, to be building, praying, visualizing, and focusing on what you can do to make the transition an effective one. You should always be focused on the light, even in the dark.

One of the problems you may encounter in the transition phase is that some people can and will be selfish, attempting to make you feel guilty about your decisions. You have to accept now that some people just won't understand your choice to abstain, and they won't understand or accept your choice to sacrifice. You may miss birthday parties, special events, vacations, showers, and so on. You'll have to ask yourself what it is that you really want out of this process. Is this change really worth risking these relationships? I can tell you right now that it is! Because the people who truly love you and want to see you win; those who want to see you happy and succeed, will understand and they will be there when you come up for air. Your true friends will be there cheering you on at the finish line. Those who are envious, selfish, and unforgiving will try to make you feel bad about your transition. God will slowly but surely begin to reveal those who no longer deserve a seat at your table. I'm here to tell you that there's nothing wrong with wanting growth. There's nothing wrong with wanting and striving for what's already destined to be yours. Be led by your spirit when people try to condemn you for changing. You can still love and respect people while loving and respecting yourself. When you're in transition, don't be afraid to take the necessary time you need to do what's right for you—or let go of those who refuse to accept your desire for greatness.

Finally, the Adult, Reproductive Stage

After you have eaten up all the knowledge, shed all the negativity, and made a commitment to achieving your goals, it's time to see the results. The amazement, the glory and the beauty of a butterfly finally shows. The butterfly looks completely different from the caterpillar. It has long, new legs; long, new antennae; and, most importantly, beautiful, brand-new wings to fly! It may be a slow start, and the transition may be tough, but I guarantee you it will all be worth it. Trust me, you will benefit from focusing on you for a change and leaving other people's thoughts and opinions of you in the dust. After growth, the beautiful butterfly can see, travel to, and experience things it never could as a caterpillar. The butterfly has a completely new perspective on life.

So, ask yourself, are you satisfied with where you are in life? Are you stepping into your greatness? If you were to leave this earth today, would you be content with your eulogy? Life is always evolving—you should be evolving with it.

Are you willing to be the amazing person I know you can be? Everyone has greatness inside of them. You just have to be ready to fight for it. Are you willing to change for the life that's waiting for you? Are you willing to drop the negative people who are holding you back from your God-given destiny?

I'm not saying that you have to completely isolate yourself from all your friends, your family, and the world. There are some cases when I do because I need to reflect solely within myself for peace, honesty, clarity, and guidance. That may not be the case for you. I'm just saying that you deserve to be around positive people who love and support you. You may be blessed enough to have a circle that's extremely supportive, but there are a lot of folks who don't. Again, this is all about discernment. It's about really looking at your life and doing a thorough inventory check for who's contributing to your life in a positive way and who's contributing to your life in a negative way.

This doesn't mean you have to pick up the phone, call the person and say, "Hi, I no longer want you in my life." Well, technically, I've had to do that for a few people. There may be a few cases in which you have to be bold and straightforward with people, especially for those who are abusive or causing an extreme amount of distress. But for the most part, just focus on living your best life. Once you begin to change, the people that don't belong will just fall by the wayside. The toxic relationships will fall apart or dissolve. Just focus on becoming the best version of you, and everything else will work itself out.

Find the confidence to draw the line and create a new standard for your life. Once you find that confidence stand strong in your new decisions. Listen, some people have serious dysfunctional issues that hold them back from loving others and treating people with respect and kindness. People are hurting in this world and we have to recognize that. Your spouse, your kids, your boss, your mother, your best friend, or your coworker didn't wake up this morning and say, "I think I'm going to ruin so-and-so's life today." Some people can't give you what they don't have. Your mother and father may not know how to be the greatest parent because they didn't have great parents. Maybe your spouse can't be monogamous because that wasn't modeled in his/her home. Maybe your best friend is always competing with you because he/she has low self-esteem. Sometimes you want something from someone who is physically incapable of providing it. So it's up to you to recognize that, draw your line, vocalize your new standard of living, and be confident in your choice to move toward happiness.

When you begin to walk in your light, it may be totally uncomfortable for them to be in your presence, and that's the truth. Some people walk, talk, act, think, and move in negativity. So when you begin to come out of the darkness, it will be difficult for them to watch. But I challenge you to stand proudly in your light. Don't dim your light for anyone else—continue to shine no matter what! Remember, you are the sum of the five people you are around the most; believe me when I say this! Take a look around you. Look at your inner circle.

If you are the most intelligent, the healthiest, the most ambitious, the most driven, or the only one who is financially stable, it's time for you to get a new circle—that is, if you want to grow. You have to step boldly and confidently in the circle of people you aspire to be like. Let their light shine on you. Get their wisdom, their guidance, and their knowledge. Relationships should be reciprocal; if you find that you are the only one with something to give in a relationship, maybe it's time to reevaluate that relationship. Sometimes we allow too many "takers" in our life, and when everyone is taking from you (money, energy, time, love, knowledge, motivation, and so on), how do you get refilled? The goal is to keep your cup filled to the brim and let others take from the overflow.

5
Drop the Old You

After I decided to take the route of entrepreneurship, focusing all my time on You're Beautiful Honie, I invested in a few conferences. The networking, the people, the information, the tools, the resources, and the insight was incredible. The connections alone made a tremendous impact on my life and in my business. During this time in my life, there were a lot of things and people that were questionable. But at one of the conferences, I met a speaker who changed my perception and made a lot of things clear for me. He is a sales, marketing, and LinkedIn guru. He also coaches and runs his own business. I ended up purchasing one of his packages, which included some audio files of his podcast. There was one audio file that stood out from all the rest. It describes something I believe all successful people go through at some point in their lives. It was something I truly needed to hear.

[Audio File Paraphrased]
      Have you ever seen the movie Cast Away with Tom Hanks? It's a movie about Chuck Noland, a FedEx employee who was in route to Malaysia on an assignment. His plane crashed, and he was the sole survivor of the accident. He ended up being the only one on a deserted island; he was by himself. He was there for five years in isolation. To keep his sanity, he took a volleyball from the airplane and turned it into an actual personality called Wilson.

He carried the volleyball with him everywhere he went on the island.

One day, he decided to try to get off the island after being on it for five years. He took some logs and vines and began to construct a makeshift raft. He then strapped Wilson to the raft and pushed it out into the water. It started to drift. Obviously, his hope was to be found. There's a particular scene in the movie that will give you the full concept and visual perspective of why I'm even telling you this story—it's pretty powerful.

He fell asleep while he was drifting on the raft. He woke up and noticed that Wilson was not on the raft with him. Now, again, Wilson was the volleyball he had converted into a personality. He looked out over the ocean, and he screamed, "Wilson...Wilson, where are you? Wilson!" He then saw Wilson in the water, floating away. He lunged into the ocean off his makeshift raft and started to swim out to where Wilson was, but the waves were too strong. He realized that he would lose the raft if he swam any closer to Wilson. He went back to the raft and untied a few of the vines so that he could hold on to the raft while trying to get Wilson. He started to swim out again, but this time, because he had returned to the raft, Wilson was floating even further away.

He struggled to pull the raft, fight the waves, and swim toward Wilson. At some point during his struggle, he lost his grip on the vine that was attached to the raft. Now Chuck had to make a decision. Was he going to rescue Wilson and certainly end his life? If he went out to save Wilson, he would not be able to get back to the raft, and he would die right there in the ocean. Or Chuck could return to the raft and continue on his journey to be rescued. Chuck decided to swim back to the raft, so he grabbed ahold of the vine that was tied to the raft, and cried out, "I'm sorry, Wilson! I'm sorry! Wilson!"

Chuck returned to the raft and began to weep bitterly, as though he had really lost someone. Most of you, without even knowing it, are just like Chuck when he got shipwrecked on that deserted island. You have a life that you feel shipwrecked on, and you're the only survivor in this life that you live. You're suffering from fear, loneliness, and despair and you're at a point where you want to change. You want to get off this island of despair. So you decide you want to make a change. You want to build a raft and find a way to get off this island, like he did.

Now here you are drifting in the ocean of change. The big problem for most of you that you don't realize is that while it was cool and good that you wanted to get off the island of despair and that you launched out into the ocean of change, you don't want to leave Wilson. Wilson represents the old self. As you grow and as God moves you further and further out, closer and closer to where he wants you to be, closer to your promised land, closer to freedom and abundance, and closer to happiness, joy, and peace, Wilson is going to want to go with you. Wilson, the old you!

There is going to come a point when you and Wilson get separated from one another. You are going to dive into the ocean of change and get stuck between the raft of deliverance and Wilson (the old you), and you're going to have to make a decision. One of them is going to drift away. You are going to have to make a decision to let one of them go. Unfortunately, most of you are going to swim out to Wilson—the old, familiar you—because that's what you're comfortable with, that's what you're familiar with. Then you will drown in the very ocean of change that was supposed to take you to your promised land. That's terribly unfortunate. Now, a few of you will do what Chuck did. You will turn back and get on the raft that's taking you to the Promised Land, and you will mourn the loss of your old self. And that's okay. It's okay if you mourn the loss of who you once were. There is no way that you can be both. You can't be the old you and the new you at the same time. There are two different mind-sets, two different attitudes, two different processes, and, most importantly, two different lifestyles. You have to let go of the old you—you have to let it drift away.

  There will be moments when you don't want the old you to drift away because you will feel the change happening inside, and it may scare you. Who is this new person coming up, rising up in you? You may not understand it right away; it may be totally unfamiliar to you. So there you'll be, swimming in the ocean of change, struggling to get your Wilson and bring it back to the raft. There has to come a point at which you realize that you can't take Wilson with you. You have to let go.

If you really want God to deliver you to your promised land, you have to let the old you go. You have to let go of your old habits, your old thinking, your old relationships, your old job—you have to let go of all of that old stuff. All those familiar things, the things that you can navigate through without thought, have to go. You are going through life doing the same old things on autopilot. Wilson has to die in the ocean of change for you to be able to be delivered to the Promised Land. Again, it's okay if you mourn the loss of these old things.

It's okay because it's scary when you're out there all alone. Yes, alone. You lost your companion, your comfort zone, your Wilson. Now you have to be out there and be truly alone, really trusting God now. There is no more crutch; you have to trust God. You have no other choice. So when he made the decision to leave Wilson and was screaming, "I'm sorry, Wilson! I'm sorry!," what he meant was, "I'm sorry I can't take you with me." He was saying, "As much as I want to take you with me, I have to keep moving forward. I want to live, and I don't want to die this way."

Chuck had to mourn the loss, and most of you need to mourn the loss. You need to go that route; you need to feel that committed to your process. Yes, there's a whole lot of risk. He was taking a risk either way. The ocean of change may have sharks, strong currents, and unknown dangers; we don't know what's out there. When you are out in the ocean, there's nothing and no one, just water and sky. There will be times where you're just out in that open water and won't know how long it will be, but you have to trust and believe in the process.

You must begin to learn how to let go of your Wilson and trust in the process, trust in your raft, and trust in God. He will send in the rescue crew. A rescue party will come to get you and take you where you want to go. You will have to make a decision to get on board with what God has planned for you or to not get on board. If you are doing the same thing, going to the same places, and hanging out with the same people, you are holding on to your Wilson. If you are not stretching yourself to learn new things and grow, you are holding on to your Wilson. If you have gone to a conference or seminar and received or purchased materials that you still haven't read, you're holding on to your Wilson. If you're holding on to an abusive relationship, you're holding on to your Wilson. If you stay at a job you hate when you know you have talent, you're holding on to your Wilson.

Let go of your Wilson. He has to die in the ocean of change. Chuck turned the volleyball into a personality so that he could maintain his sanity. That's what some of you all are doing. You are clinging to your Wilson, your old way of life, your old way of thinking in order to maintain your sanity, to feel a sense of familiarity. You're in the circle of saneness, running through the field of familiarity, and it's going to cost you. The great enemy of your progress is the familiar. The greatest adversary you will ever face is not how hard something is, not the challenge, not the work. Rather, it's the uncharted territory that you're afraid of, that will cause you to turn back to where you came from.

Let go of something—let go of something about you. Let it just drift away in the ocean of change, never to be seen again. Let something go today. You have to let something go today. I may not know what it is, but you know what it is. And you have to let it go. If you keep on holding on to it, you will drown, and you will never get to where God wants you to be. It will be a sad day—a truly sad day—when you do drown. What will drown with you will not be just your hopes and dreams. You're interconnected to so many other lives that need you to make it. They need you to be found and rescued from where you are. [End audio file]

(Larry Beacham, "Wilson," *The Champion Builder Webshow* (audio blog), accessed July 20, 2015).

In the end, Chuck was found. The risk he took was worth it. He had a new life, just like you will. Your life will be better—better than you could have ever imagined or comprehended. Don't fall for the old you, don't fall for your past life; be 100 percent committed to moving forward. Be cautious and aware of even the smallest step back. I remember every time I thought I was over my ex, he would try to pull me back in slowly and subtly. I would allow a phone call or lunch, not really thinking of the consequences. I was continually sabotaging the healing process. Stepping, slipping, and eventually falling all the way back in to my old life. It wasn't until I fully let him go that I was able to heal, gain my confidence, and become a new person. You have to learn how to enjoy and be committed to the new person you're becoming.

You know how a new relationship feels, right—the courting process? Everything is fresh and new and just feels so carefree. This is your opportunity to drop the old you and begin courting the new you. Fall in love with building this new relationship with the new you. You can create yourself to be anything you want. Buy yourself more books, go to conferences, and network in your field. Treat yourself to a mental-health day, embrace your new attitude, love on the new you, go to the spa, and buy yourself that new jacket! Begin to treat yourself the way you want other people to treat you. This is an opportunity to set a new standard for everyone in your life; past, present, and future. Sometimes people don't feel like they need to treat us with love, respect, and admiration because we don't treat ourselves that way. Don't be afraid to let the old you go and to get excited about the potential in building a new you.

6
Drop Negative Places

Negativity doesn't just come from people. It also comes from places. We all know we have some places that encourage us to lose self-control or maybe even to lose our minds. Your intentions may be pure, but when you are placed in a certain scene, it's hard for you to control your impulses. It's a trigger—a trigger of emotions, actions, and feelings. It's a trigger of desire and longing, of hunger and cravings. It may be a trigger that is directly correlated to the advancement of your relapse or backsliding way. We all have triggers, weakness, and temptations, but it's our job to be aware of those triggers and respond accordingly.

Certain places just aren't conducive to your well-being. You may have places you still like to go to "have a good time," but for some reason, going to these places continues to wreak havoc in your life and causes issues for you. There are levels of enjoyment, right? There's joy, a good time, fun, and immense pleasure. And then there's obsession, addiction, and lack of control. Everyone has a vice. We are all flawed. We have bad habits and shortcomings, and we all sin. No sin is greater than another, and no one is perfect. But on this journey toward change, accountability, success, and good fortune, you must be honest with yourself when it comes to these imperfections. Whenever we're trying to change or break habits, it can be hard in the beginning, but it's up to you to have self-awareness. My mother used to tell me all the time to "avoid the very appearance of evil." That's what the Bible tells us. It says to separate from, abstain from, and avoid all things that are evil. We all know what places will cause us to stray off our paths to greatness. Don't be afraid to acknowledge them.

There are some places you can avoid and some places you can't. Let's explore a few "places" that had an impact in my world, and what I had to do to change them.

My environment, where I lived

I walked away from an environment that was toxic for me. Although I had a lot of people, family and friends that I loved in South Jersey; I just couldn't see myself striving there. I was connected to too many things that were negatively impacting my world. There was a lack of motivation and inspiration there. I didn't know too many people in the area that aspired to do the things I wanted to do. I felt stuck, I was suffocating, and I wanted to be free—so I moved. Moving is one of the single most drastic things you can do to change your situation immediately. It automatically forces change in so many areas of your life; and for me that was a good thing. I had a fresh start, a new lease on life. Placing myself in a new environment changed everything. Yes, I was scared. Yes, I went through some rough times. Yes, I was lonely at first. Yes, I was angry with friends and family that didn't visit. I often thought if I went back life would be so much easier—less competition, less responsibility, and less pressure. I'd be an average adult—working, living, paying my bills, and just existing. I couldn't, though! I knew I wasn't "average," and neither are you! I knew God called me to do something more, and I was on a journey to find out what that "something more" was, no matter how crappy I was feeling. The hope of what was to come trumped all of those emotions.

    As I began to mature in the new environment, I began to grow into a new woman—and that was confusing as well. It was so unfamiliar, and to be honest, it felt weird. This new Lena was different. She didn't talk the same, walk the same, think the same, or carry herself in the same way. All because she changed her environment. That experience, the transition, was frightening. One day, I cried to my love, he always keeps me grounded. I was so afraid of losing me, of losing sight of who I was—the little brown girl from Camden. I told him, "I don't know who this woman is yet. I don't know who I'm becoming. What's her style? How does she measure up? Is she bold? Is she still silly and fun? Who is she?" He laughed and said, "You are her! You can't and won't lose the things that make you who you are, the things that make people love you. Your intelligence, your beauty, your essence, and the way you treat people—those things matter most. Your morals and values, those things have never changed. You don't have to know everything right away, right now. You have the ability to create and build the woman you want to be." He pulled me right back from the ledge, as he always does.

    In that moment, I realized that I wasn't the same woman I had been, four or five years earlier, and there was nothing wrong with that. I took pride in knowing I made the right decision to change my environment. One move changed the entire trajectory of my life. I'm not saying the answer to all of your problems is moving, but I can guarantee that placing yourself in more positive environments that are conducive to your growth and goals will change your life for the better. Now, let's look at some less dramatic examples of places I had to avoid when on my journey. As I share my stories, think about some places you may want to frequent less.

Malls, department stores, online stores and outlets
We live in a consumer society in which the buying and selling of goods and services is the most important social and economic activity for many people every day. There were times in my life where I made so much money, and I look back and just wonder where it all went. I used to be so irresponsible with money. However, that mentality changed real quick when the market crashed. I learned the hard way. I see a lot of people use money as an excuse for why they can't go back to school, can't save for their own place, can't put their kids in private school, or can't start their own business. But when you look at their lives you see them spend money in the most irresponsible ways. Consumerism is a lifestyle. You have to look at your finances and be more realistic about your future and what you want. You can't live in the mall and then complain about not having enough money to pay your bills. Take a look at the following

questions, and think about where your mentality is concerning material items and shopping.

- Do you constantly compare what you have to what other people have? Do you do so to the point that you are unhappy, depressed, or unfulfilled because you can't have some of the things that other people have?
- Are you in debt? Have you always been in financial trouble or been unable to get out of financial ruin because you're trying so hard to keep up with the Joneses? Do you purchase items that you know you can't afford just so the items can be seen by your friends, family, and peers?
- Have you done this so much that the debt doesn't even bother you anymore, or do you have so much debt that you can't sleep at night because you're thinking about how you're going to get out of it?
- Do you have an emotional attachment to material possessions?
- Are you the type of person who's never satisfied with his/her life and lifestyle no matter how successful you become? Are you constantly focused on getting to the next level (a new car, bigger house, or more clothes) that you forget to enjoy what you already have?
- Do you feel that you must keep up with the latest trends or people won't respect or like you?

- Do you often sacrifice family time, social time, and special events because your only focus is shopping? Are you an impulsive buyer?
- When you get paid do you find yourself going straight to your favorite stores?

If you answered yes to any of these questions, you may need to reevaluate the way you shop. If you have an impulse, a trigger, or a weakness to buy things when you go to the mall or shops, maybe you need to take a step back and ask yourself why. I grew up in an environment in which people purchased name-brand clothing, expensive jewelry, and designer handbags but didn't own any property, have life insurance, or college funds. I had to completely re-wire my thought process around consumerism.

Take control of how you spend your money. Instead of "wasting" money learn how to earn it, protect it, and grow it. Invest in yourself! Go to a professional/personal-development class, become a member of a networking organization, take a class that could help you expand your business, buy some life-coaching sessions, invest in your child's talents/hobbies, or take a financial wellness course. Don't waste your money on menial things that won't have a positive, progressive impact on your future. Shoes, clothes, handbags, gadgets, and trends won't take you to a place of financial freedom. You have spending power. Who are you giving that power to?

Restaurants and fast-food joints

This is a tough one, because in America everything we do revolves around food. We eat for every celebration, every festivity, even for leisure and fun. It's a subject I know all too well being a city girl with a southern family. When I was working in New York City, eating healthy had to be a conscious, planned, and intentional decision every day. Literally! The city is just filled with yummy goodness up and down every block. No matter where you go, there are just incredible restaurants and food everywhere. Making healthy decisions wasn't always easy for me. Two words "Happy Hour!" Ridiculous specials on great food, amazing drinks, music, and friends—in one of the greatest cities on earth! It's a disastrous recipe for unhealthy living, but who can turn it down?

Seven years ago, my focus wasn't on healthy living. Stress was a trigger and food was my comfort, so my weight yo-yoed up and down for years. I had no health conscience then. However, once I put my focus on healing I learned the importance of nutrition, fitness, and my overall wellbeing. But as you know, striving for health and fitness in the society we live in today can be hard. This is especially true because we're a working society, where many of us spend most of our day sitting down. This is not good! So here are a few tips that helped me out while I was striving for change.

Make it clear to your family and friends that you're striving towards a new path. Try to limit the amount of times you eat out during the week and choose places that have healthy options. Listen, I know I'm an impulsive person that loves to eat. So there's no going to Buffalo Wild Wings and ordering a salad for me. You have to be honest with yourself. If my boyfriend orders macaroni and cheese, more than likely I'm going to have macaroni and cheese. It's all about knowing yourself, what you want, and being vocal with your loved ones about the changes you want to make. Again, if they love you, they will be willing to help you adjust and make the necessary changes.

If you're like me, there may be some times where you have to use avoidance until you can build up your tolerance and self-control. I would literally take the back entrance and walk down the next street behind my job to avoid passing the pizza shop. I know, it's a little crazy, but I had to! Why? Because I knew that at least half the time, I couldn't resist the aroma of fresh pizza and garlic. I knew that if I ended up walking past that pizza shop alone, I'd probably go in for a slice, justifying it as a little snack before dinner. Now, if I had done that three or four times a week, I'd be in trouble. So, I altered my actions and avoided it all together. Getting off the train, I knew which corridors to exit to avoid passing the Cinnabon counter, which was even worse than the pizza temptation. This may sound elaborate and extra, but if it's what you have to do to reach your goals, so be it. What's the alternative? Caving in to your old lifestyle, starting your journey over every Monday because you couldn't avoid the fast food joint? You aren't in competition with anyone else but yourself. My will power sucked at the time—end of story! Day in and day out, I had to be aware, put in the effort and make conscious decisions about the choices I made. After a while I started going to this deli that had healthy choices. I'd order egg white, avocado, tomato, and swiss on wheat for breakfast, or I'd grab a salad for lunch. Eventually I didn't even miss the pizza shop. I would walk by and hardly notice it half the time, because I made the sacrifice to build my tolerance.

So if you need to drive down a different street to avoid the burger joint, do it! If you have to get up a half an hour earlier to prepare your lunch so that you don't fall into the lunch trap at work, do it! If you need to walk an extra block to get around the pizza shop, do it! This is your life. Don't worry about what people will think or say. If it's getting you one step closer to your goal of healthy living, then it is worth it. Again, we have to do something different to evoke change in our lives. To get results you've never gotten, you've got to do some things you've never done—even if they are a bit unorthodox.

I know that changing your diet can be extremely difficult, trust me I've been there. But it's all about prioritizing and knowing what you want out of life. We cringe at spending fifty to a hundred dollars a month for a gym membership, but we will splurge on appetizers, entrees, drinks, and desserts at a restaurant. I know it's what you're used to but you can suggest different activities when spending time with your loved ones. Go to a workout class instead of happy hour; go jogging, take a boxing lesson or spin class instead of a big brunch. Get active and have fun. There's so many other ways to socialize.

Nightclubs, casinos, and bars
    If these places are getting in the way of your happiness, you should definitely drop this habit. I've seen people lose it all because they couldn't handle the responsibilities that come with adult nightlife and entertainment. I've seen families torn apart because of financial ruin due to excessive gambling. I've seen marriages dissolve because of the lifestyle that comes with frequenting nightclubs and bars. This is a matter of self-control. Of course it's important to enjoy your life and take part in activities that bring you happiness. But at what point do you realize it's too much and it's having an effect on your relationships, health, finances, and/or social life?
    I love to party! I love to have a good time, and I enjoy entertaining others and being social. It's what I do. I'm an only child, so I grew up always wanting to have the company of others. In my twenties, I did a lot of clubbing, partying, and vacationing with my girlfriends. I lived five minutes from Philadelphia, forty-five minutes from Atlantic City, and two hours from DC and New York—there was no shortage of a good time when I was coming up. I really can't say that I missed out on anything. Celebrity after parties in Las Vegas, pool parties in Miami, Caribbean parties in New York, mansion parties in Los Angeles—I've done it all. But when I began to establish myself, my brand, and my

company, I realized my partying habits had to change.

I was buried in projects, finishing up my master's degree, and building a foundation for my business, all while watching my friends continue to live it up. It was tough at first. I always felt like I was "missing out" on something. However, I began to get super focused. I was focused on my future and advancing to the next level. I became less concerned with nightlife, being on the scene, and attending the parties. At some point, I didn't even want to spend money on seeing the same people at the same parties. All I wanted to do was invest in my company, so I began to choose my entertainment wisely.

It's called growing up! Instead of spending money going to the clubs and bars every weekend, buying outfits and shoes, spending money on bottle service, and paying for other forms of entertainment (ie: concerts, sports games, happy hours, gambling, and so on), I chose otherwise. Don't get me wrong—I continued to enjoy my life, but it was within reason and with a purpose. I partied with a purpose. I socialized with people who could add benefit to my life. I traded in partying for networking. I joined a professional development organization and took on a few leadership roles with the executive team. I started to "party" in environments that would foster productivity and growth, not just in my personal life but in my business as well. I began associating myself with people of influence and spent my money on events at which I could actually learn and grow. Instead of going to concerts, my new thing became conferences. Instead of pointless happy hours, I began to attend social mixers that had an agenda or provided a guest speaker I could learn from. I still enjoyed myself, but I had grown out of the pointless partying.

    In no way, shape, or form am I saying that I don't party or go to nightclubs anymore, because I still do. I choose wisely, and it's way less frequent. I see people I grew up with still doing the same thing, going to the same places, and partying with the same people. As I became more and more of a public figure and brand, the less I wanted random people in my personal affairs. Even if you're not building a business, you may be trying to build relationships, build your marriage, advance in your career, or be a better parent. In all of those scenarios, you will need to prioritize accordingly when it comes to your time and where you spend it.

    Today, everyone is watching, all the time. It may not seem like employers and contractors care about your personal life, but a lot of them do. They look on your social media accounts to find out how you let your hair down and/or spend your leisure time. With social media being so prevalent, you have to be extremely careful of where you're going and what you're doing. If you're out there hanging in places you shouldn't be and someone snaps a photo of you doing something silly or records a video of you, it could jeopardize your job or business. Whether we accept it or not, we're being judged, and everyone has a camera phone to aid in their judgment these days. A huge part of success is all about branding, perception, and what people think about you. I just learned how to be more careful about the places I frequent.

There are just certain sacrifices you'll have to make in order to attain success. These sacrifices may be different for different people, in different industries, with different aspirations. But nonetheless, I guarantee you, in order to break through to the next level you will have to make some changes. Please, don't drown in that ocean of change. Fight through the layers of discomfort.

I just shared a few examples of "dropping" places to give you a small perspective on why it's important to change your environment. But I'd like to share a big accomplishment I made when it came to "adding" places. There was one particular experience that served as an amazing teaching tool for me. I taught me how to choose places that would provide a long-term, constant impact on my life, oppose to going to places that would provide a short-term, fleeting impact on my life. So, when you "drop" something negative, don't forget to "add" something positive.

Let's jump right in. I had no idea how to play golf or why it was so important in the business world. To be honest I had no clue how people could tolerate the complexity of the game. All I knew about golf was that men spent long days and big bucks at country clubs to enjoy it. Growing, all I could see was the cultural and economic reasons why black people didn't play golf. A basketball is significantly cheaper than a set of golf clubs, and there were no country clubs in the urban communities I grew up in. It wasn't until I started going to the Boys & Girls Club that I was personally exposed to sports like tennis, golf, and soccer, and even then it was at a basic level.

    Well, on my journey of change, on which I surrounded myself with new people and immersed myself in new environments, I ended up attended my first golf outing. The day consisted of working alongside two golf pros; practicing driving, putting, and chipping; and, if you were good, playing a full course. I didn't play the course, but I took my time and learned the methods, techniques, and strategies of playing golf. One of the first dates I went on with my boyfriend was to a driving range, so I was familiar with that aspect of the game. However, I was clueless in regards to everything else.

    Talk about being out of my comfort zone. I was terrified! I was so worried that everyone else knew what they were doing while I simply had no clue. All our lives we're taught to look at fear and failure with a negative perception. Your outlook on life, your emotions, and your mentality are strongly dictated by your perception and what you were raised to think or feel. I had to shift my thinking and look at this as an opportunity to grow. Although I was nervous because I didn't know what I was doing, I had to realize that's what the golf clinic was for. It was to help people learn and grow. If you look at fear as an opportunity to learn and grow, you won't be so afraid.

    Stop letting fear, failure, and the unknown hold you back from accomplishing things you've never done before, going places you've never been, and socializing with people who could change your world. Adding *new* positive things to your world is a must. What if I had said, "I'm not going to the clinic because I don't know how to play, and I don't want to embarrass myself?" I would have missed out on a perfect opportunity to expand my network and knowledge base. I would have thrown away an opportunity to learn some new things about myself and about the game. Plus my partner plays golf, so now I'm able to go out with him, hit a few balls, and share a few laughs. I expanded not only my knowledge base but I also expanded an avenue in my relationship. You never know what doors are going to open when *you* are open to new things. I'm going to share some of the life lessons I learned from playing golf, and by no means am I a pro, but you don't have to be to take something great from the sport.

Lena's Golf Lessons
Integrity
Everyone scores his or her own game, and each player has to call his or her own penalties. People expect you to be honest about what you're doing and how you're scoring yourself.

- Who you are inside is important. Your morals, values, and character, no matter what the scenario, matters.

Time Management
Golf can be an extremely long and tedious game. It's important for you to always be on time. If you are on time, you are late.

- There's always a broken traffic light, an emergency phone call, a detour, or an unexpected delay. Be mindful when people are waiting on you; it's important for you to respect their time.

Pressure
When you're playing golf, there can be an immense amount of pressure. Golf teaches you how to slow down and get focused. When you are prepared for and focused on what you're doing, the pressure will subside.

- Life can sometimes present pressure, nervous energy, and anxiety. Practicing the art of calm and focus could be the difference between you living a life of peace or one of stress.

There's a Time to Play…and a Time to Play!
There may be some drinking, socializing, and fun going on during a round of golf. But when it's time for someone to step up and play their turn, they usually get serious.

> •There's no problem with having fun and enjoying yourself in life, but you have to know when it's time to step up and take care of business!

Know Your Craft
People spend a lot of time off the course practicing. Golf is a really tough sport. No one goes to one clinic and expects to go out on the course with people who've been playing for years.

> •When you set out to switch industries, start a business, or follow your dreams, respect the craft. Learn all you can about the industry and surround yourself with the greats. This doesn't mean you should sit back or be passive. It means respect and learn from those who came before you.

Learn from a Mentor
We learned from a pro—a leader, a mentor, someone who could help along the way.

> •When learning and growing, and we all need encouragement, expertise, and accountability. Don't be afraid to reach out for help when it comes to perfecting your craft.

Awareness
If you know your best drive is 80 yards and your putting is bad, you may not want to go out to play a serious game with pros. Be honest with yourself. You don't want to delay the game and hold up their day. Remember, it's all about respect, etiquette, and integrity.

- Self-awareness is key. We have to be honest about our capabilities. Don't tarnish your reputation by biting off more than you can chew. I'm a huge advocate of taking risks, stretching yourself, and setting audacious goals, but it's important for to also be calculated. If your goals aren't realistic, attainable, and task oriented, you could be setting yourself up for disappointment.

Networking
Golf is also about establishing trust and relationships. There's a lot of business done on the golf course, so it's a great place to establish connections as well. But you don't want to be the sore thumb who stands out as being there solely for business and not for the sport or camaraderie.

- When networking opportunities arise, be smart and make sure you're taking a genuine approach. You should be looking for commonalities when getting to know someone. It's about making and keeping a connection.

Adversity
This is no easy game. Golf takes focus and precision in a way that I've never experienced. It takes practice and requires a lot of multitasking. You have to think about your feet, your legs, your waist, your arms, your elbows, and the wind among other things. There are just so many different variables, it's extremely tough. People who have been playing for years still say there are things they could work on. Golf is about perseverance.

•In golf you will face adversity and obstacles, but pushing through is key. You have to be able to play your way through sticky situations and be steadfast in completing the course. That's how life is. You have a bunch of things to manage and a bunch of unknown variables that come out of nowhere. You have to make the decision to keep going, keep pushing, and see your dreams through until the end.

There! I learned all of that just from sticking with golf. This was just one example of me taking a chance and doing something I wasn't comfortable doing, something I knew I wasn't good at, something I wasn't exposed to as a child, and something that is known to be a challenge. Can you just imagine what other experiences, wisdom, knowledge, and opportunities lie on the other side of discomfort? It's imperative that you learn how to step outside of your comfort zone and start adding new things to your life that are positive, today!

Don't hold yourself back with complacency. You will be surprised at how much your life will change once you start going to places that are different, more positive, and productive. It's all about changing the scenery and stepping into the life you really want. Walk in it as though you're already living it! Life is about experiences and moments. What fun is it without change? Why would you want to do the same thing day in and day out for years at a time? I understand that some people are completely satisfied with where they are in their life, and they simply want nothing more and nothing less. But if you're reading this book, I take it that you want something more. I can't speak for everyone, but changing my environments changed my life.

7
Drop Negative Things

It's not always easy to identify the negative things in our lives that keep us from excelling. As much as we hate to admit it, it's easy to identify the people who negatively impacting our world. These people hurt us, judge us, disrespect us, lie to us, put us down, and show us a lack of support. They may try to mask it with love, smiles, and gifts, but that doesn't change how we feel. Our emotions provide us with clear warning signs and red flags. Even when it comes to places, we know where we should and shouldn't be hanging out—it's fairly simple. It's a feeling of conviction, like backsliding with the ex. We all know right from wrong deep down inside. However, when it comes to "things" we can be a bit more passive. It's not always as straightforward, black and white, or noticeable in our lives.

Anytime a person is fully dependent on something, it can be extremely difficult for them to identify the negative influence of that thing. This may be one of the hardest chapters to accept and implement. I'll be covering just a few prevalent things that people suffer from. This is often where we see a loved one reach out and try to help. So, I'm hoping that if any of these tendencies ring a bell for you, you will seek assistance. There is absolutely no shame in reaching out for help—I've been there. The shame lies in living with the pain. You are not alone in this world, and there is nothing that you're going through that someone else hasn't already gone through and survived.

Substances, Activities, Lifestyles, or Situations
    I don't believe in highlighting one thing or another when it comes to addiction. Addictions can range from drugs and alcohol to food, work, sex, and gambling. There have even been studies that show people experiencing extremely high levels of stress and anxiety when separated from their phone for too long. Anything can have a hold over a anyone if they allow it. I'm not here to judge. I know people who have suffered from addiction—losing their lives, marriage, children etc. I just hope that if you're dealing with anything of this nature, this book moves you to let go of whatever it is that may be controlling you.
    Sometimes people know when something's controlling them, other times they have no idea. In their mind, everything is fine and well, while on the outside everything is falling apart. After seeing my father struggle with nicotine, I do believe it's one of the hardest addictions to overcome. I never knew if he understood how much power the cigarette had over him. I watched him go through a near-death experience, struggling with throat cancer. He quit smoking for a while, and then started back up a few years after remission. He continues to try, lord knows he does, but it's still a struggles. Amidst scary doctors' visits he'll stop, and then shortly after he'll start again.
    I don't know what's worse—the kind of addiction that leaves you without family, friends,

money, dignity, health, and peace or the kind that allows you to fully function and believe that nothing you're doing is wrong. Most addictions generally begin very subtle. If you are doing something that's beginning to rob you of your happiness, health, wealth, finances or mental stability, don't be afraid to get the help you need. Life is a gift; you are a gift. We all struggle at some point, and this section of the book is about facing that something that has taken control of your life.

      Have you seen a change in your performance? Have you seen a change in your ability to focus? Does this thing cause you to have a lack of motivation or desire for the positive things in your life? Do you feel depressed afterward, as though you wished you'd done something else with your time, energy, and money? Do you sacrifice time with your loved ones to participate in or enjoy this thing? Are you experiencing physical deterioration? Has there been a change in your physical appearance? Are you losing sleep or sleeping too much? Are you losing or gaining weight? Does this thing force you to leave everything in your life—friendships, opportunities, and dreams? If so please seek the appropriate resources.

      Keep in mind, as I said before, an addiction isn't just characterized by substances. Deep down inside it's the emotional attachment and emotionss we're connected to that makes us enjoy this "thing" that controls us. These questions remind me of myself several years ago. I was so in love with a man who was totally unavailable—in more ways than one. He led me on for years; it was a terrible, codependent, obsessive mess. I knew he wasn't good for me, but I was so addicted to the dysfunction of it all. I enjoyed the breakup-to-makeup emotional torment. I didn't care what the feeling was as long as I could feel. I gained weight, lost weight, cut my hair, I settled, and cried myself to sleep many of nights. I willingly engaged in the public humiliation of it all. When I was in it, I couldn't see the problem; the inability to let it go was so damaging. I was truly addicted to the pain, to him, to the relationship. For some strange reason I found it comforting. Although I knew it was a hot mess, I knew what to expect. Looking back, I can't believe I enjoyed that time in my life. It was literally like a soap opera, but I craved it. I loved the drama. As long as I was in it, could feel it, and was a part of it, I was cool.

    The truth of the matter is none of that was healthy. When you are addicted, you allow something or someone else to control your life. Having a dependence on a substance or activity isn't beneficial to your mental, physical, or emotional health. If you cannot function one day without this thing and find yourself having a compulsion or fixation with this thing or activity, you may need to seek help. In order to change things in our lives, we have to face them head-on. It's not your spouse's fault, your kids' fault, or your parents' fault. The responsibility is yours. Start by finding out how and why you fell into this position. Addictions, compulsions, and fixations aren't just a result of habit. Remain confident in your ability to change your habits.

Mental and Emotional Scarring
Did something happen to you a long time ago that you just won't face? Is there something that is too difficult to think about? Has someone physically, mentally, verbally, emotionally or sexually abused you? Are you trying to hide that pain? Do you take that pain out on others? Have you suffered significant loss in your life? Does your promiscuity or sexual addictions come from some early childhood experience or a form of sexual abuse? Do you abuse substances to avoid reality? Are you hurting?

Those are tough questions right? Questions that made you uncomfortable. Questions that so many of us are afraid to answer. Questions that I ran from for years. It's not so much the questions that give us the chills, it's the answers. Because so many of us have either experienced these things or know someone that has. Although the answers to these questions can leave lasting scars on us, it's important to know that the future can be so much brighter when you make the step towards healing. There is freedom in acknowledging the answers to these questions and facing them without fear. We all have dark spots in our past, but it's up to you to choose light, today and every day moving forward. Don't let the past dictate your future. You have a God-given right to have joy in your heart, peace in your soul, and love in your life. Allow your past to be just that.

This book embodies so many first steps towards healing, however you have to find your own path to making things right. Who do you need to forgive? What family conversations need to be had? What therapy do you need to move forward? Who/what do you need to eliminate from your life? What responsibilities do you have when it comes to atonement? Do you even want healing? These are questions you have to ask *yourself* before moving forward. The healing lies beyond these answers. Burying the pain doesn't solve anything. Later on in the book I will go into spiritual growth. Sometimes a supernatural presence key to our healing, and I will help you develop that growth.

Interpersonal Relationships
I often see addiction closely correlated with interpersonal relationships. Most people are introduced to new things by someone they know, like, and trust, whether it's a partner, friend, or relative. Again, you are the sum of the five people you are around the most. If your boyfriend or girlfriend has a problem, you may develop that same problem. Your friends and whoever else you spend a great deal of time with will have an influence on your experiences and choices. It's up to you to make the right decision about the people you surround yourself with.

Then again, some of the things we do are a result of what we saw growing up and how we were raised. We can't escape our parents or how we were raised, but as we get older we can take responsibility for our own lives and make better decisions. If your parents had horrible eating habits, weren't active, and didn't take care of their health, you may have inherited some of those same traits. People like believe things like high blood pressure, high cholesterol, diabetes, and heart disease run in their family. In some cases those things are truly hereditary, but often times it's the lifestyle that's been past down. If bad habits and tendencies are rubbing off on you, try your best to create respectful boundaries with people. Especially when you're on a journey to finding the new you.

Sometimes we don't know how we develop these bad habits; these "things" we do. But deep down inside we know ourselves, we know our weaknesses, we know our vices, and we know what will cause us destruction. So don't run from them, acknowledge those things that may cause you harm. You have to know what and who they are in order to abstain. You can't fix a problem you don't think you have. Once you acknowledge those things you can create a whole new life by making new choices, doing new things, meeting new people, and going new places. But you can't walk into a new life with old habits, old ways, old lies, old flames, old lovers, old ideas, old thinking, or the old you! You just can't.

It may seem like a huge feat at first; to just let go and let God—but I encourage you. Even I look at His tasks for me sometimes, and I'm simply overwhelmed. There have been times when I've questioned my purpose, my power, my capabilities, and my faith. Looking at the vision He has for my life, I wonder if I measure up. Then I realize that he's not asking me to do anything He can't help me do. As long as He resides in me, I possess the power to achieve anything I set my heart to; and so do you. I get excited knowing that He will move the universe to make it happen for me. I believe that when you commit to greatness and hold up your side of the deal God will do the rest. He will put you in the right place, at the right time, with the right people; that will bestow bountiful provisions in your life. Just remember, your desire for change creates an energy that gets the attention of the universe. But it's your actions that initiate the shift. There is no person, place, or thing that can stop you from achieving greatness once you've committed to that shift!

8
Change

I know—it's a lot, right? Change this, change that, change everything! No one likes it. I didn't like it at first either. I just told you to get rid of some pretty important people in your life, stop going to places you thoroughly enjoy, and drop the things that bring you pure ecstasy. Whether you want to admit it or not, you know deep in your heart that some of those things or people are holding you back from achieving your highest potential. You have to make an intentional decision to change and to be ready to deal with the emotions that come with it. I know. It's scary. Nothing's predictable, everything feels uncomfortable, and you may even feel like you are suffering a bit. The key is getting through that stage. You'll have to fight through by staying encouraged, reading, writing, and praying or meditating. Be resilient. You have to acknowledge that the new you is worth fighting for. Once you get to the other side, you will look back and realize that everything's okay. You don't have to have all the nerve, all the courage, and all the answers right away. Just be willing to take the first step, and then the next, and the next.

    I didn't have all the answers. Excuse me—I still don't have all the answers. But I'm willing to make a move whether I have all the answer or not. You'll never know it all. This quote from Francis of Assisi is at the end of every newsletter I send out, because it's how I live: "Start by doing what's necessary; then do what's possible; and suddenly you are doing the impossible." Just start. Do it today! Try, believe, do, go, make an attempt, and put forth some effort. No one expects for you to have it all mapped out perfectly or get it all right on the first try. At least I don't, and you shouldn't. But it is important for you to take a step in the right direction, and don't look back. Focus on forward motion.

I am in a place now in where everything in my life is different—all the time. I don't fight it. I don't have the energy to fight every uncomfortable moment in my life. I've learned to embrace it. Believe me—it's like a snowball effect. Once you allow change, it will constantly occur; and once you learn how to deal with it, you will get better at handling it. If you want better finances, better relationships, better romance, a better environment, a better lifestyle, higher intellect, and more opportunities, you have to get out of your comfort zone. It's not always pretty out there, in "uncomfortable town," but you can handle it.

I held on and tight in times of depression, times of abuse, times of homelessness, times of distress, times of financial ruin, times of loneliness, times of heartbreak, and in times of brokenness! Just because I decided to turn my life around doesn't mean I'm exempt from hardships. I hold on to my faith and declared that for every negative there is a positive. I understand that change is a part of the process, the journey, the voyage. When I was in transition I just focused on living in the moment, I never looked back. I knew the life I wanted to live, and I knew I had to remain committed to change in order for things to get better. Before I knew it, my entire life flipped. I was healed. I was in a thriving, healthy relationship. I had new family and new friends. I became a public figure, held two seats on an executive team for an elite national organization, and founded a nonprofit. I traveled to places I had never been before, I wrote this book, I began the healing process with my mother, and I helped countless other strive towards the same success. I accomplished so much more in such a short amount of time because I *allowed* change into my life. Don't fight it. Several years ago, none of what I have now existed! None of it! I am a brand new me.

      Maybe you haven't asked yourself lately, but who are you? Who do you want to be? How do you treat people? What kind of energy do you put out into the universe? Does who you are now match up with the person you'd like to be? Sometimes there has to be a change in you before you can begin to change your situation. You have to take a long look in the mirror and acknowledge your character flaws. No one wants to work with, be in a relationship with, or be around someone who carries negative traits. Your personality, character, energy, words, and attitude matter. Take a look at the following chart. Be honest with yourself about what characteristics or traits you may have in the right column and how you can begin to change those to more positive traits like those in the left column.

Traits of Happy, Successful People	Traits of Miserable, Unsuccessful People
Patient	Hasty
Kind	Rude
Has self-control	Acts on emotion
Loyal	Untrustworthy
Generous	Selfish
Peaceful	Messy or petty
Humble	Arrogant
Grateful	Entitled
Forgiving	Holds grudges
Loving	Careless
Supportive and encouraging	Unsupportive and discouraging
Accountable	Blames others
Celebrates others	Criticizes others

Traits of Happy, Successful People	Traits of Miserable, Unsuccessful People
Embraces change	Fearful of the unknown
Express true emotion	Suppresses emotions
Thirsty for knowledge	Has no aspirations
Read, meditate, visualize, and journal	Consumed with TV, media, or socializing
Always willing to learn	Thinks they know it all
Works well with others	Confrontational
Focused	Has no direction
Sets and attains transformational goals	Never has a plan
Helps others to succeed	Self-absorbed
Learns from mistakes and appreciates the experience	Fears failure and scared of making mistakes

People often forget how important character is—our morals, our values, and our standard of living says a lot about who we are. A huge part of fulfillment comes from our interactions with others. Purpose and fulfillment are often tied to family traditions, raising children, being a good person, giving back, and shining bright so that others are inspired. It's about leaving a lasting impression on those you love. So there's no shame in having room for improvement. We could all use a little tweaking when it comes to our attitude and/or personal character traits. Again it's about having a strong self-awareness.

People will try to make this hard for you. They will constantly remind you of who you were. They will constantly bring up what you did in the past. They will tell you that you'll never change. They will remind you of all the times you failed to change. People will feed you a recipe of lies that will have you questioning your ability to change and grow. They will have you ready to give up, surrendering to their truths about you. But I challenge you to create your own truth about the new you. Those who don't have the strength to change will try to stop you from obtaining the life of your dreams. Stay away from those people. Continue to refine your character and make the nonbelievers choke on their lies about you. Take pride in the new you.

When you are faced with naysayers, tension in your circle or an ounce of self-doubt here are some things you can do to push forward.

Faith

You, most importantly, have to believe in the change. Your thoughts are the first line of defense. You have to think it, visualize it, read about it (in self-help, inspirational, or personal development books and materials), and talk about it (with those you trust, who are supportive and encouraging). Your mind has to be receptive to the change—allow it to be! It may be strange at first, believing something you don't feel is true, but go ahead and drink the Kool-Aid. Believe in the unseen as though it is. Have faith in your ability to stick with it.

Honesty

Don't be afraid to be transparent. Be open; say to yourself and others, "I may not be there yet, but I'm working on it. Each day my goal is to work on me, step by step, day by day." Maintain a sense of integrity so people can respect you, your new choices, and the steps you are taking toward happiness. Take it slowly, achieving what you can one step at a time. My everyday prayer is, "Lord help me be a better person today, than I was yesterday." By no means am I perfect, but I'm trying. That's all anyone who loves you can ask of you—is that you try.

Perseverance

Being committed to the process of change is necessary. It takes courage to walk forward in the new you. It takes confidence to believe that you can be this new person. This process will require you to have strong determination and tenacity. Walk in it, allow the process to stretch you. Don't give up. You can't win if you're not even in the game. Stay in it.

Restraint

People are going to test you. They want to see if you're really going to change for the better, if you can really succeed, and if you really have what it takes to maintain the change. The trials and frustration will come, so practice self-control. Don't lose the new you by reverting back to the old you; remain prudent. Stay focused on the future, and be wise about your reaction to the nonbelievers. Don't give them any energy; that's exactly what they want. Reacting would be proving them right. Practice the art of restraint, keep your vision clear, and stay focused.

Accountability

If you slip up, it's okay. Acknowledge it and move on. Be honest with yourself, and be careful of pointing the finger. Take the time to figure out where you stand in a situation before placing blame on someone else.

Light

Give light! Show that you truly exude the embodiment of your higher power. There should be an aura about you; your spirit should shine! You should be a walking testament to optimism. People should be able to look at you and see the evidence of belief. Your life should inspire others. Don't just change with the intention of changing just because.

Change with the intention to find and walk in your purpose. This entire book is about you getting up, taking charge of your life, and stepping into your greatness. Every religion that I have encountered teaches us that there is a higher power that dwells within us. You have to tap into that power, seek it, and let it shine. Ephesians 3:20 says, "Now to him who is able to do immeasurably more than all we ask or imagine, according to his power that is at work within us." His power—that is at work within us. His power is my power, his light is my light, his peace is my peace, his abundance is my abundance, and his love is my love. His divine light should shine right through you. Your presence should feel like a gift, because it is. When you believe and operate in this thought, negativity will slowly disappear. I wouldn't even know if I had haters, because they're not my focus. There are people who live in drama and there are those who live above it. Be someone who lives above it.

Judge No Man
When your life begins to change, you may begin to look at those same haters with a different eye. Don't give in to the temptation of judging others for remaining the same. You may have made the physical changes, environmental changes, and financial changes, but where it matters most, is in your heart. It's not your place to judge. When you judge someone, you are creating an invisible wall that says your way is right and the other person's way is wrong. You are saying, "I am superior and you are inferior." Don't do this. It's wrong.

Changing your life (in search of happiness, healing, love, success, peace, and so on) doesn't make you any "better" than anyone else. It's simply a choice. A choice you can't force on anyone who doesn't want it themselves. You have to remember everyone has a different idea about what happiness and success look like; and you have to respect that.

Deepak Chopra says that everyone is doing the best they can with their current level of awareness—let that sink in. *Your* current level of awareness may have been expanded by reading this book. We are all at different levels, and none of them are better than another. Your happiness isn't a representation of everyone else's happiness. Don't change, and then look down on others, or start to force your new lifestyle on your loved ones. This will cause unnecessary conflict. It's great to encourage them or guide them in the right direction if they ask, but be considerate—think about where you were when you started.

9
Roll with the Punches
Learning to Have Unwavering Faith

The Smoke

In some cases, before you can even feel the heat or see the flames, you are confronted with smoke. The dense, foggy cloud inhibits your ability to see clearly, making you disoriented, confused, and fatigued. In most fires, people don't die from heat or burns; they are killed by smoke inhalation. Toxins, fumes, vapors, and particles penetrate the respiratory system shutting it down, taking life with it. When you feel like you're being overcome by the billowing toxins that fill your life; use faith, clarity, and vision to clear the smoke. Don't let a lack of spiritual connection rob you of reaching your highest potential, achieving your dreams, finding your purpose, and transcending to a higher level with your creator.

Sometimes we exert all our energy fighting instead of just rolling with the punches and having unwavering faith. Do you find yourself worrying about every little thing that happens? Do you get into arguments about the most ridiculous stuff? Are you a person that gets yourself all worked up when things don't go your way? Do you fret over things you literally have no control over? Life is too short. It's too short to spend anytime stressing about anything. If you can change it, get to work, do your best, and be satisfied knowing you did. If you can't, let it go, give it to God, and exercise your faith. Simple as that.

Each day when we wake up, we have a choice to be happy, to let things roll off our backs, to smile, to enjoy our lives regardless of the circumstances, to operate in love, to be grateful, and to simply roll with the punches. Some of you don't know how to do that, how to be free. But it's okay, because you're going to learn here. Life can be a battle sometimes, and in some scenarios we have to fight. Life dishes out some incredibly tough blows, but you have to know how to deal with them. You have to learn how to maneuver.

Let's look at the greatest boxer of my era, the undefeated champion Floyd "Money" Mayweather. It's funny; people either love him or hate him, but they can't deny his talent, which always speaks for itself. Floyd has been listed in Forbes magazine as the highest-paid athlete of all time, but how many people know or care about his childhood? People are way more intrigued by the cars, women, money, and private jets in his life than they are about his challenges.

Floyd grew up with a mother who struggled with drug addiction and a father who sold drugs. He makes it no secret that his life was hell growing up. He talks about how difficult it was to take care of his family once his father was incarcerated and how hard it was losing his aunt to AIDS. Floyd is a man of great experience, yet he lacked education. He was a high-school dropout and began fighting professionally at a very young age. Early on in his boxing career, Floyd learned a technique that would eventually make him famous, a concept that left people fascinated—that would build his legacy. The technique was his a strong defense.

Floyd Mayweather gained the nickname "Pretty Boy Floyd" as an amateur. After fights, Floyd would have very minimal scarring, and he wasn't one to take a lot of punches to the face. Why? His defense is impeccable. Floyd has mastered some of the best defensive techniques out there. But there's one in particular, the shoulder roll, that he does so well. If you've ever seen this man fight, you know that it's truly a sight to see. This line of defense is incredible and has become a highlight in his career. Floyd, is the king of rolling with the punches. If you don't believe me just google it.

When life throws a punch your way, you can either put your fists up and block it or put your shoulder up and roll with the punch. I'm not a boxing expert, but just "roll" with me on this one. When I refer to "blocking," I mean having both fists up in front of the face. Most often we see this when a fighter has been hit hard and begins to retreat while his opponent goes on the offensive and begins to pummel him. When I refer to the "shoulder roll," it's more of a protective stance, I'll go into the detail of the stance later. For now, let's look at why "blocking" life isn't the best option.

When We Block Life's Punches:
This is when we oppose something or someone in our lives with force, when we hinder life's natural ability to teach us a lesson, when we object and fight ourselves on the journey to becoming better, when we are disobedient to the word of God, or when we refuse to accept a tragedy, loss, or circumstance and label it unfair. In life, this is called *resistance*. When we block/resist life experiences or use all of our energy fighting people, we lose. To block a punch, you have to put up your fists, and when you put up your fists, a few different things happen.

1. You impair your line of sight when you block. It obstructs your vision and you aren't able to see your opponent. Remember, this section of the book is about gaining clarity in life. You can't go through life with your fists up all the time, constantly blocking everything. Some things are just meant to happen, and when you try to block them, you're only hindering yourself. Being able to see things clearly is a huge advantage, but how can you achieve clarity if you continue to block every experience that will teach you to see things from a different perspective?

Often times when you look back on a situation you can see everything clearly. You can see where the problem was, how you messed up, or where someone betrayed you. But while you were in it, you couldn't see anything! You have to fearlessly practice the art of awareness, always being able to see what's happening, and learn from what life's blows.

2. You will intensify the impact of the blow. We are all human; it's natural to have a reaction when life's hitting you hard. However you have the power to control how. You control your emotions, your feelings, and your responses to all of life's circumstances. Will you be hurt, angry, and disappointed? Will you be damaged, depressed, and suicidal? Or will you accept the truth, try to let go of the past, and move towards healing?

When you fail to accept the things that you can't change, you are only intensifying the pain— causing yourself to feel even more agony. Life is going to strike, period. There will be things that happen in your life far beyond your control or your capacity to change. When these things arise, you have to be able to recognize them and accept them for exactly what they are. This level of recognition, understanding, and regulation falls under emotional intelligence. See, all of our emotions derive from the same energy; it's our job to intellectually categorize them appropriately—for the sake of our mental and emotional health.

3. You create a false sense of security when you hide behind those gloves. A part of you thinks you're safe—for a second, you believe you're protected. People try to block the pain all the time with things or substances. While they're drunk, high, or shopping, in that moment, they think they're safe and secure. They feel good, they've blocked the pain. They've found an opportunity to temporarily escape. But when they come down from that high the pain is still there. You can't hide behind the gloves, you have to deal with life head on.

When life hits you—POW—and you put up your fists, blocking the punch, you didn't throw life off. Life expected you to hide behind your gloves, resisting, crying, putting off, disobeying, and feeling entitled. So guess what? POW—again and again! Because what you resist will persist. You are predictable; life knows you well. Putting up your fists is like mocking life, saying, "Ha-ha! I can block you! I'm secure." But really, you are setting life up to treat you like a punching bag, because you are still, unchanging, and settled in your ways. You aren't proactive, just reactive, putting your opponent in a better position. You're not even prepared to counter efficiently and effectively.

Now, let's look at the alternative. Facing life head on, being prepared, strengthening your line of defense and countering strong!

When We Roll with the Punches

When we shoulder roll we do not resist life's trials. We go with the flow. We accept life's challenges and learn from them. This is when we allow people to be themselves without trying to change them. It's learning to control your emotions and understand that everything in life is orchestrated. Nothing's a coincidence; it's all ordained. It's being aware of who you are and not allowing the actions of other people to sway your character. It's being obedient to God and trying to live a life that He would be proud of. That's rolling with the punches!

When you shoulder roll, you are not cowering. You're protecting yourself and setting up your countermove. It's defense at its best. The stance is as follows.

- Left shoulder high and chin low—protecting the face/head
- Left arm/hand across the stomach—protecting the body
- Right arm/hand up and across the chest—protecting body/head and preparing counter

When you roll with the punches, things happen a bit differently than when you block.

*1. You have a clear line of sight.
The shoulder roll gives you the ability to keep your eyes on your opponent at all times, so you can be prepared for action.*

There is nothing more enlightening in life than being able to see and accept things for what they truly are. When you can see things clearly, you can prepare, execute, and move efficiently and effectively in life. Focus on seeing the truth in other people, in situations, and, most importantly, in yourself. If your spouse is a liar and a cheater, stop making excuses for them and accept them for who they are. If you know you're at a dead-end job, recognize it, devise a plan, and change your career. If you are overweight, accept that as the truth and work towards the things that need to be changed. If you think denial/blocking is going to help you in the fight of life, guess again. Being able to see clearly and be honest with yourself is the key to freedom.

*2. Rolling with the punches saves energy.
Rolling gives you the ability to adapt to any situation; it's a more relaxed way of protecting yourself.*

When you see Floyd Mayweather fight, he makes it look so effortless, as though he's just sparing for fun or something. He never looks flustered or exhausted. You have to learn how to choose your battles wisely. You don't always have to try and fix, change, and control everything. You have to learn how to relax, let go, and let God. Stop exerting all your energy, and give it to him. Let him do the work. Let life get tired of shooting the jab and never landing a punch.

3. The roll is difficult to penetrate.
When your chin is down and your left shoulder is high, you are protecting your face. When your left arm is tight and close across the stomach, you are protecting your body. The other side is turned away from your opponent, and your right arm is high across your chest, protecting and preparing to counter. Where can your opponent go? Nowhere! They can only get off short, small hits or a complete hit and miss; nothing's clean. Do you know how beneficial that is to a boxer? No head injuries, no long-term damage, and quick recovery times. I'm mean really, let's think about it, how many times has Floyd Mayweather been knocked out?

That's what life is all about: being able to take some hits but never getting knocked down! Wouldn't you love to be in a position in which you could never be knocked down in life—not by your boss, the tire that blew out on the highway, your cheating spouse, the test results from the doctor, the house fire, or the failed business? I'm not saying we shouldn't care or acknowledge our emotions. I'm just saying that no matter what happens in life, if you are still physically here with breath in your body, and you are alive to face it, then you have a chance to turn things around. When you build up your protection with strength, resiliency, self-esteem, faith, clarity, and vision, you can handle anything! No hit will knock you down.

4. You quickly throw your opponent off. When you do a shoulder roll, you change the conditions of the fight. Your opponent realizes they missed, so mentally they're thrown off. They weren't anticipating the miss, and now they have to re-strategize. They may even take a stumble with that miss, which puts you in a better position. A person can't recover as quickly when they hit, miss, and stumble. But if they landed the hit because you had your hands up blocking, they could continue hitting you repeatedly.

You have the capability to change the conditions of your life by choosing to respond to things differently. If you try to not let things bother you, they bother you less. It's as simple as that. If you spend more time focusing on all the good things in your life and all the things you're thankful for, more of those things will show up in your life. If you show, give, and operate in love, more love will come to you. If you operate in generosity, more generosity will be displayed in your life. If you operate in frustration, anger, and resistance, that's what you'll reap. Change the conditions of your life by shifting your energy. Throw people off; don't respond to their games, their attitudes, or their negativity. Kill them with kindness. Be so unrecognizable that they have to go out and find someone new to play their childish games with.

5. You can counter quickly.
When you shoulder roll and your opponent misses, changing the conditions of the fight, you are no longer on the defense. You've shifted swiftly to the offense. When you have both your fists up to block, you're still on the defense—where your opponent still has the advantage. This, ladies and gentleman, is why Floyd "Money" Mayweather is undefeated. His shoulder roll is so smooth that once his opponent misses, it provides the perfect opportunity for him to come in with that right hand and land a strong punch.

When you let someone else control your emotions, you are giving that person power over your life. Don't get knocked down! Anticipate the punch, roll the shoulder, and come back with a strong jab. Accept that things happen, and remain calm and always be in control of your emotions. POW! Declare that you will overcome. BOOM! Understand life comes with trials, learn from the lessons, and vocalize more affirmations. WHAM! See people for who they truly are by accepting their actions. Don't try to change them; forgive them and adapt accordingly. BANG! Recognize your own faults, take control of your life, and implement action steps toward change. BAM! Counter life! Counter strong! Show life that YOU are in control of this fight. Show your opponents that you will never hit the canvas. Every time you do something that brings you peace, happiness, and understanding, you're countering life. The more practice faith, optimism, and belief in yourself, the more comfortable and confident you'll be with your offensive strategies in life.

Final Thoughts
Think about some of the ways you can roll with life a little bit better. There are so many things that we can just let go, not argue about, and move on from so that we can make our lives better, happier. I've been on a conscious and intentional path of self-improvement for many years now. My demeanor is extremely laid-back, and there's not much that can really get me worked up these days. When you've been through some of the things I've been through, you choose not to create battles where none exist. Creating happiness is my focus.

You have to come to a place in your life where you are truly unbothered by the outside world; a place in which you can automatically clear the smoke and toxins from your world. If you let external factors determine your life, you'll never be happy—in a relationship, at work, within your family unit, or in general. Remember, ships don't sink because of all the water around them. They sink because of the water that gets inside them. Internally, you have to stay cleansed; don't let people, things, limitations, opinions, criticism get deep inside you. Focus on the positive.

Know yourself. When you are an honest person, you're not moved by liars. When you are sure of yourself, you won't be hurt by envious people with low self-esteem who try to bring you down. When you work hard and take pride in your gifts, you won't settle for less. When you value yourself beyond the physical, you won't let your body stop you from serving a purpose in this world. Stop giving your energy to the bad thoughts and emotions, and just focus on the good ones. Don't hold on to a negative feeling or emotion. Feel it, recognize it, accept it, respect it, and move on to a more positive thought. Don't dwell in it, live in it, or allow it to fester. Let it go!

      Practice the art of control. When you learn how to become more aware of what's going on, your actions and your responses, things change. Most of the time how we respond typically depends on how we see things. So, clearing out the smoke in your life, having clarity, and connecting internally, will change how you view things, how you process events, and how you respond. Clarity (the ability to see things clearly) controls perception (the way you understand or interpret things); which in turn has an impact on your choices. So, don't be afraid to take step back, let some things go, and just roll with the punches. It will truly make for a stress free life.

10
What Do You Believe?
Getting to faith

Some people's dreams, aspirations, and goals are destroyed long before they even attempt to achieve them because they have no sense of faith or belief. There's nothing deep down in their spirit that pushes them. They aren't connected to their source. If you are going to attempt to do anything great in life, anything different from what you're currently doing, you have to learn how to operate in your faith, whatever that faith is for you.

I've been exposed to and have practiced several types of religions. Quite frankly, in my experience, they are all very similar in nature. When you strip most religions of their practices, traditions, and cultural systems, their skeletons are the same. They all teach a way of life (good versus evil, positive energy versus negative energy); how to treat other people, belief in a higher power, and a notion that says that you can do anything with that higher power.

I hope this section of the book leads you to a stronger personal relationship with your higher power, a new level of spirituality, and a heightened connection to the universe and everything in it. I want you to connect on a deeper level, to connect spiritually with the power that resides within you. For me, religion and spirituality are two separate things. Religion defines a particular category of belief systems (ceremonies, rituals, practices, worship, cultural beliefs, traditions, guidance principles, and so on). For some, it's a way to define who they are. It's a way to show the outside world that you operate within a particular set of beliefs. Spirituality, has nothing to do with anyone else but you. It has nothing to do with what church you go to, what you wear, or how you pray. Spirituality is personal. It's about connecting, listening, and harnessing that energy that lies deep down inside of you—your moral compass.

    There are thousands of established religions in the world. The one you will be a part of will generally be determined by your environment: what area of the world you were born in, what religion your parent's practice, what culture you're in, and what social circles you choose to get involved in as you get older. I was raised as a Christian. There are about 7 billion people in this world, and about 2.2 billion people identify with my faith. Now, within Christianity, there are well over forty thousand denominations. You can be Catholic, Baptist, Methodist, Lutheran, Presbyterian, Protestant, Pentecostal, Mormon, Jehovah's Witness, Evangelical, Orthodox, Seventh-Day Adventist, or Apostolic and still be a Christian. Some of the denominations are very similar, and others are extremely different, calling for different practices, beliefs, and ways of life. So I've always looked at Christianity and thought, "Wow! Within 'my religion,' I could still be following the 'wrong' practices and traditions. And if I can be "wrong" within my own religion, who am I to judge others for believing what they believe in? I've never been one to judge people based on their faith.

So when I say religion *isn't* personal, it's because we show our practices and ways of life *externally*. What *is* personal is your individual, *internal* relationship with God (whatever you believe to be the source of all power and creation). It's your ability to connect with the universe and all things in it. I won't be the one to sit here and tell you that my religion or belief system is superior to yours. The important thing here is that you develop a stronger belief in who you are and your abilities. That you understand the importance of morals and values on your journey, and develop a sense of security, faith, hope, and trust. These are the foundational things you will need when walking in your greatness. It doesn't matter to me how you get there. Once you begin to seek it, you will find it.

People often try to use religion to separate and divide. But I find that experiencing different religions has brought me even closer to God, because of the connection it allowed me to have with others. Being open gave me the ability to connect with people from all around the world—roommates, classmates, coworkers, and clients. I'm able to connect with people of various backgrounds because I don't draw a line, I don't judge, and I'm proud to say that I live a life of inclusion. Exploring different religions has taught me so many great life lessons and has allowed me to grow immeasurably in the spirit realm. I operate on a much higher level than I did before because of that exposure. I've also learned a great deal of life lessons exploring and being exposed to various religions.

I was introduced to Buddhism at a very early age; I was about fourteen or fifteen. My best friend at the time, and high-school sweetheart, was a Buddhist. So as you can imagine, I was exposed to the culture, practices, and worship techniques on a daily basis. I went to the meetings and of course I experienced a lot of chanting . Although he is no longer with us, his mother and I have always been and always will be extremely close. She is one of the greatest spiritual mothers I have. She has helped me grow in ways that I can't even begin to articulate. Her influence has helped me become the woman I am today. She gives me that sense of clarity when my life is filled with smoke and cloudiness. Her strength, her guidance, her wisdom, her aura, her spirit, her personality, and her love are simply divine. She extends her gifts far beyond family and friends; she is a mother to the community as well.

  She introduced me to the Buddhist faith and their practices but never pressured me to convert, change my ways, or who I was. She simply kept the door open for questions and always welcomed me with an invitation to the meetings. After attending a few meetings, I realized I knew more people who practiced Buddhism than I thought. It's all about keeping an open mind and heart to things you feel in your gut are good. Why would I push her out of my life or not accept her for who she is and what she has to offer just because she communicates with God in a different way than I do? I would have missed out on years of love, laughter, and comfort in my times of need.

I never felt awkward or out of place at their meetings. I grew up in a church where people spoke in tongues; so it wasn't uncomfortable to hear multiple people chanting at meetings. Nam-Myoho-Renge-Kyo is a chant of dedication. It's a path to finding higher enlightenment. It's understanding that the universe is based on cause and effect. A life of practicing Buddhism is a life of abundant wisdom, courage, compassion, and empowerment. It's a religion focused highly on gratitude and understanding that the power of the universe lies within. I remember the first time I heard it, the chant. It was so fluid and sounded more like humming than words. It's very relaxing. It puts you in a trance, and I find myself reaching back to that practice when I'm experiencing high anxiety. I've learned a lot from Buddhism, and I actually enjoy it. It's calming and pure, and the practice of meditation is incredible. Plus, being one, in your home, in front of your own altar (the Gohonzon), is powerful. That's it—just you and the universe on a quest to achieve greatness, peace, and abundance. In this crazy world, the practice of Buddhism brings great calm and peace.

What I admire most about Buddhism is the dedication to prayer. Much like Islam, prayer is a huge part of the religion. It's something they do all day, every day. I've learned a lot from my family and friends who are Muslim as well. They live a life of sacrifice, obedience, and humility; all in dedication to family and heritage. They are some of the most pious people I know. Growing up in Christianity, I experienced a lot of inconsistency.

People prayed over food, prayed when someone was sick, or prayed when they were in difficult times, but I didn't see a lot of daily prayer. Buddhists and Muslims, make it a habit to pray multiple times a day. It's like breathing to them. I believe staying in the face of God through prayer and meditation is extremely important, because the closer you are to him the easier it is to hear his voice and see things clearly.

Most of the Muslims I know are extremely dedicated. I look at their actions during times like Ramadan, and they are so committed. I look at myself and wish I grew up with that level of discipline. Don't get me wrong—I understand that these are just my experiences and that people of all religions are human, good and bad. I'm just sharing what I've learned in my experience of accepting people from different religions; it's important not to shut them out on your journey but instead to see what could be gained from their experiences and knowledge. I have learned so much from sharing my life with others and gained so many life changing experiences from being open to learning new things about different faith systems. I use various practices to encourage clarity, healing, and closeness with God—from meditation and fasting, to reiki and the use of anointing oils.

I grew up in the Pentecostal faith, which is extremely strict. Later on, by choice, I was baptized in and attended a Baptist church. Unfortunately growing up I witnessed a lot of people "playing church." It was all about what you were wearing, who had the best voice, and the collection plate. A "good" church had a stellar choir, a performing pastor, and folks that could speak in tongues and shout on queue with the band. But when I was at my lowest point in life, I found myself questioning these practices. I was going to church week after week, month after month—and nothing was happening. I wasn't growing, my spirit wasn't being fed, I wasn't being healed, and I wasn't getting the tools or resources I needed to change my situation. After every service I still felt empty and unfulfilled. I still felt myself searching for answers. I knew, deep down in my heart, there was so much more to my life. But at the time I was depressed, confused and wondering how I ended up on my best friend's couch, escaping an abusive relationship. I knew that there was no way in the world this was the life God had planned for me. So I began to dig deeper.

With faith, religion, and spirituality you have to seek the answers for yourself. You can't be passive. Go search for the answers to those burning questions. I wanted to know what my life's purpose was. Why I was here and where was I headed. Would I leave a legacy? Would I ever establish a stronger relationship with God? Would I leave a footprint on the world? Where was my true potential? How much more could I handle? What could I do to build my strength? Living on that couch was the best thing that ever happened to me. I had to be at my lowest point to seek God the way I did. To search for a church home the way I did. To become the obedient servant I try to be today. But you don't have to wait for that low point; you can make the choice to seek God/faith today.

I needed to find myself and find God. I believed that He would lead the way, but I didn't know how to listen to him. I believed that this source of power existed, but I had never truly tapped into it. I knew how to pray, but I didn't know how to listen and have faith beyond my current existence. I knew how to praise and worship, but I didn't know how to have complete peace and joy no matter what the circumstance. I knew what it meant to be a good person in life, but I didn't know what it meant to have purpose. So I began my journey of connection, spiritual growth, emotional intellect and true love.

I stopped going to church for a while. I needed an opportunity to seek God on a fresh new level. See for me, at the time, church was like icing. We all like icing, right? It's sweet, it comes in different flavors, different colors, and it covers up any imperfections on a cake. But what's icing without the cake? Your spirituality, your belief in something greater than you, your oneness with God, your ability to allow God to order your steps, your faith, inner strength, and moral compass should be the cake.

Your connection and personal relationship with the source should be at the very core of all you do. It should be your foundation and the very essence of who you are. People should be touched by you, your presence, and your gifts. Church or your religion and practices should be the icing on the cake—accentuating your personal connection to God. It should elevate you, provide you with support, and allow you to give back and have an impact on others. A close personal relationship with God combined with a healthy church family, should provide you with the strength, encouragement, faith, and purpose you need to create long-lasting positive change in your life. Don't give up, give in.

11
Learning to Connect

I keep talking about connecting—what does that mean to you? Does it even exist in your world? Maybe it means nothing. Maybe all this religion, belief, connecting, higher power, God, and faith stuff means nothing to you. Well, I challenge you to believe. Even if you think you are connected, I challenge you to strengthen your relationship with Him, Her, and/or The Universe. Whatever you believe your higher source of power is, I challenge you to clear out all the smoke in your life and see clearly. I challenge you to use your mind, body, and spirit to tap into that source. This is where the real change happens! When you clear, heal, and build the strength and power of your mind, body, and soul, miraculous things happen in the physical and spiritual world. As I break down some of the techniques I used in my journey to strengthen my connection, take notes on what you can use to strengthen these areas of your life.

Mentally

Meditation
How often do you take quiet time for yourself? How often are you alone with no noise, no kids, no spouse, and no distractions—just you? This is extremely crucial in the connecting process to gain clarity. The answers to most of our problems can be found simply by connecting with our inner self. Unfortunately, today we have so many distractions and responsibilities that focusing on

you may seem selfish or impossible. But the truth is you have to take care of self-first before taking care of anyone or anything else in your life. Clarity in all your new choices and decisions will come from your ability to find the time and opportunity to connect with your inner self.

We work toward that connection by practicing things such as meditation and prayer. Meditation is a mental exercise that allows you to reach a heightened level of spiritual awareness. It's an opportunity for you to exercise important mental-health practices. Meditation can help with a variety of mental-health issues, such as stress, depression, and anxiety. It's a way to rest and recharge your brain. Meditation is a strong mental practice that is known to produce significant change in people's lives. There is no right or wrong way to meditate. If you begin to research, you will find complete variations of all types. Some people enjoy light calming music while some people prefer to meditate in silence. Some people believe you should clear your mind; others feel like it's okay to have a few thoughts as long as they're not overpowering the moment. Some people will chant a mantra, while others recite affirmations. You should do whatever you find most comfortable, effective, and empowering. Meditation is for the benefit of you, so find the methods and techniques that bring you the most peace and build from there.

Personally, meditation has been an on-and-off battle for me. It requires a certain level of focus and concentration, which for me means constantly battling my thoughts, emotions and time. It's a continuous journey for me, one that I haven't perfected the way I'd like. My mind runs a million miles a minute without brakes, so it can be tough for me. But when I do get into a flow of consistent meditating, it works miracles. It's a huge help, and it keeps me grounded. Oprah and Deepak Chopra have various guided meditation series that are absolutely phenomenal. These guided meditations are much easier for me to follow, and they help me remain consistent. I truly enjoy them. Meditation gives my mind an opportunity to rest and revamp which is extremely powerful.

Prayer

Prayer, for me, feels more like a conversation with God—I never feel alone. It's an opportunity for me to express my thoughts, desires, concerns, and thanks to the Lord. You may not always get the answers you want right away, but if you listen close enough, you will often hear what you need to. When you transcend closer to your higher source of power, you will be able to hear, feel, and see things you never have before. You will witness miracles in your life, windows open where doors were closed, and favor beyond your imagination.

Prayer truly confirms God's presence for me. I am empowered in knowing that my requests are going to the most high. In my experience, when I put a request (a prayer) out into the universe (to God), I create a powerful shift, and God begins to move people, places, and things in my direction to fulfill that request. But you have to remember that once you've prayed you have to have faith that your prayer will manifest. And then you must operate as though you already have it. You can't just drop your prayer off and say, "Okay, see you later." Because again, it's a conversation. God may be speaking to you, telling you to do something, go somewhere, or take action that will lead to the manifestation of your prayers. If you're not faithful, optimistic, and willing to listen, you may miss your blessing.

Prayer comes in all forms, just like meditation. Whether you chant, bow, kneel, sing, or dance, let your prayers be heard. Don't let anyone tell you that you must do them in any particular fashion for God to listen—he's always listening. You can talk to God however and whenever you like. You don't need to speak the King James English for God to hear you. Prayer comes from you, from your heart, so just be genuine. Don't let anyone define the relationship you have with your higher source of being. That's personal.

Knowledge

Your mind is the most important and powerful organ in your body. You should be taking care of it and exercising it every day just like you take care of anything else. Proverbs 15:14 says, "The heart of him who has understanding seeks knowledge, but the mouths of fools feed only on folly." You must seek knowledge, understanding, insight, and awareness to see clearly and have clarity. Clearing the smoke in your life may require you to seek knowledge in many forms. It could be school, conferences, learning from life experiences, spending time with those who are wise, or immersing yourself in new environments. These are all amazing ways to seek knowledge. When you open your eyes, you'll be able to learn something new from every experience, every day. It's important that you choose the pathway to knowledge that best suits you. For me, reading seemed to be the most beneficial during my journey of understanding and growth. It provided me with a totally different perspective on life and opened my eyes, my spirit, and my mind to so many new things.

     I consistently read and study the Bible. You can find incredible strength, encouragement, and wisdom in the bible. For me, it provides an outline of how I should go in the way of the Lord—it's my moral compass. It demonstrates how I should walk, talk, and treat others. It helps me in times of distress, confusion, and pain. It brings me great joy, healing, and hope for the future. The word of the Lord has kept me sane in times I know I would have lost my mind.

     In addition to books that strengthen your spirit, choose books that strengthen your self-confidence, help you hone in on your purpose, and become an expert in your field. Reading will bring you closer to your dreams in a more intimate way. Me personally, I'm not always moved by colorful speakers—the ones that scream and holler at you, jump up and down, and run across the stage to get their point across. I've been to more conferences, symposiums, boot camps, retreats, conventions, and seminars than you can imagine. I thrive off of personal, private, and intimate awakenings. Reading allows me to receive a message in many different ways. I can read a book over and over again, and each time I read it, I receive something new depending on where I am in my life. I hope this book serves that same purpose for you.

Purpose

If you are still searching for your purpose, you should consider using all of the mental exercises (meditation, prayer, and reading.) When we mentally clear our minds of all the clutter, big decisions and revelations, such as our purpose, become clear. We're able to see opportunity with a new set of eyes. Listen, you only have one shot at this. That's all. You only have one life to live, to create greatness, to leave a legacy, and to fulfill your destiny. If you haven't begun searching for why you are here on this earth and what you're supposed to be doing, you should start today. God placed us all here for a reason. We are all gifted and talented beings. Your presence on this earth signifies that fact, but it's up to you to find it. You will know. Your purpose will bring you so much pride and joy. It will bring you peace and happiness. It's one of those things you could do every day for the rest of your life and never get bored! But keep in mind our purpose isn't always handed to us—mine wasn't. I had to go through many trials and years of uncertainty before I bought into my gift of healing, coaching/counseling, and helping people find success.

Physically

Our Body

The preservation of our physical selves is imperative to sustaining our health. Everything on our bodies was created for a purpose, and we should respect and honor that. When your body isn't functioning properly, what goes through your mind? How do you feel? What happens when you don't treat your body right? Your body is the temple of the Holy Spirit. In many religious books, it declares that you are not your own. You are a vessel, the dwelling house of God. So why wouldn't you take care of your body? Most people aren't motivated to live a life of health, wellness, and fitness, because they have yet to take the time out to recognize, acknowledge, and take pride in all that the body does. They weren't taught how to respect the body, love the body, and cherish the body.

Remember, God is looking to use you; he wants to express his creativity and greatness through you. How can he do that if you are not taking care of your health? I'm not just referring to the obvious toxins like alcohol, nicotine, and drugs. I'm talking about actually taking great care of your body—watching what you eat, making sure your body is active, and getting enough sleep. The human body is such an unbelievably amazing machine. It heals itself. It alerts you when something is wrong. It operates without you having to tell it to. Your brain, your emotions, and various chemicals are all affected by how you take care of your body. Are you taking care of your body, the way it's taking care of you?

Read up on the benefits clean eating, things like yoga, and how much rest the brain needs to function. Look at the cancer rates in countries in which they grow and eat their own foods, and compare them to those here in the United States. Go on-demand and watch some documentaries about health. Movies like Forks over Knives; Fat, Sick, and Nearly Dead; and Earthlings changed my entire outlook on what I put in my body. Your physical self, your senses, your brain, and the way your body functions should all be important to you. It's your job to take care of it. You don't have to accept the "mainstream" way of life, just because. Again elevation, success, and your journey to the next level will require you to leave some old ways behind. But in order to do that you have to seek knowledge, education, and be willing to try things you've never done before.

Experiencing Nature
I didn't realize how influential and powerful it is to be in the physical presence of nature. There's something restorative about going to a new park, taking a walk along the beach, or hiking a small mountain. On my journey, I developed a great appreciation for the little things in life—or, in this case, the biggest thing: the earth. Such a marvelous work of art. Just think about the beauty that lies in everything that has life and energy—the trees, the oceans, the flowers, the moon, and the stars. Now, think about the power and magnitude of the sun, wind, and water. Think about the variation in color, shape, size, and purpose of all that exists in our

world. Take a second and really think about it—every blade of grass, every ounce of water, every cloud, every planet. There's beauty in at all, a level of greatness and perfection to each thing; including you. You are just as much a part of that energy and life. You belong here on earth just as much as the trees, the sun, and the moon. You have just as much purpose and power! Never forget that.

When my life began to change, the opportunities to travel became more frequent. I began to see colors in the sunsets I had never seen before. I experienced pollution-free skies that allowed me to see the stars shine bolder and brighter than I had ever seen them before. As you begin to take this journey, you will start to establish a respect for everything that has life. I'll never forget one time me and my love had a picnic in the park. We turned off our phones, grabbed some food, and laid out in the grass. I looked up at the trees swaying in the breeze. I let my feet get acquainted with the grass, and we just laid there. We chatted every now and again, but mostly we just laid there listening to the sounds of the park. I remember the bees feasting on the little white clovers in the grass. But there was no swatting or fighting them off. In that moment—and in many others with my love, whether we were lying on the beach or taking a walk through the park—everything was perfect. It's almost as if time stopped. We were one with nature, not having to fret over time, e-mails, work, or anything else. Something as simple as lying out in the park can become so therapeutic. It brings such a tremendous sense of calm that we don't get every day.

When I physically began to draw nearer to nature, my life became that much more interactive. I began to hear and see things more clearly. There were no clouds of misunderstandings. Some of the answers I had struggled to find manifested when I learned to be one with nature. This past summer I was collecting rocks on the beach in Oaks Bluff, and God was speaking to me. The breeze, the water, the rocks, and his voice were euphoric. His voice was crystal clear. Those moments and experiences taught me how to feel his power.

I've had several mind-blowing a-ha moments when connecting with the earth. One happened when I was driving up the coast of Oahu, in Hawaii; another was while climbing Dunn's River Falls in Jamaica; and yet another was while looking over the Grand Canyon. These experiences granted me answers to questions, insight into the future, and confirmation of the present. What a feeling! The feeling of being a part of something as big as the mountains or as strong as water—simply unbelievable. No sirens, no horns, no loud noises, no crowds, no ads, no billboards, no distractions. Just me and God.

Maybe you've seen mountains and swam in the ocean before but weren't doing it with the intention of feeling something amazing, hearing God's voice, receiving the answer to a question, or feeling 100 percent alive. Go forth with the intention to *experience* nature instead of just seeing it. It doesn't have to be Hawaii or Jamaica. That's the beautiful part about experiencing the spirit of God and connecting with the universe and everything in it, you can be anywhere. God's with you all day every day. You're surrounded by life energy and nature every day. But when you learn how to be intentional about the experience, you will heighten your spirituality and connect with your source on a deeper level.

Find ways to connect in your everyday activities. When you go outside to take a break from your job, rejoice in the moment. Go outside, lift your head up to the sky, feel the sun on your face, stretch your arms up high, feel the breeze on your skin, breathe in deeply, and become one with the ground you stand on. Acknowledge all the elements one by one; don't take them for granted. Literally stop and smell the roses. Feel the softness of the petals, smell the sweet scent of its body, take delight in the bright pigments, and rejoice in the fact that you and the rose are alive together in that moment, one. We are alive because of the air we breathe, the water we drink, and the food we eat, which is all provided by the earth—plants live, trees live, we live. So take the time to experience nature on a daily basis, and be open to listening to your inner self.

Spiritually

No one can fully direct you on the path to obtaining a more personal connection with your higher source of power. It's something that you must have a true desire for. It's something you have to take seriously. You can't be afraid of it either, because once you begin to move forward you will see and feel things that will blow your mind. This journey of spiritual development will be personal. There's no proving it to anyone or doing it for anyone else. It's something you should take great pride in, because once you fully connect on this level, you can do anything you put your heart too. There will be no problem or situation too great for you to handle. You can go anywhere, achieve anything, and be anyone you'd like once you learn how to connect with God/the Universe. I've seen it firsthand.

When you seek God's goodness and live it every day, your life will begin to reflect it. But you have to be the reflection first. You won't get there with vengefulness, grudges, un-forgiveness, and hatred in your heart. The longer you hold on to those negative emotions that don't reflect the spirit of God the harder it will be to connect. Once you begin to operate in the spirit of love, kindness, forgiveness, and generosity, the universe will automatically begin to work in your favor.

My love and I have this thing we do whenever the universe is working in our favor. Whenever we are blessed, whenever our prayers have been answered in the most unique way, or whenever we simply manifest the desires of our hearts, we look over to each other and say, "That's the Universe!" We simply take a second to acknowledge that there is no coincidence and that God has orchestrated our paths and works miracles in our lives every day. I've had some truly out-of-this-world experiences, and I'm just glad that he's always there to witness them. Otherwise, people would think I'm crazy or lying. When you begin to walk in your path of greatness, when you commit to living a life of purpose, and when you are willing to step into your destiny, everything will fall into place. You will just know and feel the elevation in your life, it will be apparent.

I can't give you or tell you about something that you have to experience for yourself, but I can give you a few tips that will help you reach that transcendent experience. For anyone searching to make the connection, I'm going to make this really easy for you. The universe works in a very simple way. It's about belief, energy, and karma. So let's get to it.

Belief

You have to believe beyond your current situation and mental state. Building that deep, spiritual relationship with your higher power requires a strong level of faith and trust, just like any other relationship in your life. It requires your ability to let go, declare greatness over your life, and affirm that blessings are coming your way.

Philippians 4:6–7 says, "Do not be anxious about anything, but in every situation, by prayer and petition, with thanksgiving, present your requests to God. And the peace of God, which transcends all understanding, will guard your hearts and your minds in Christ Jesus." And Mark 9:23 reads, "Everything is possible for one who believes."

You have to give faith an opportunity to work in your life. Allow your higher power to show up in your life. You may not be acting in a manner that allows God to show up. For instance, when you are dating someone and begin to make things exclusive, how can you trust that person if you never allow him or her to be in a position to be trusted? It's the same thing with God. If you sit at your desk every day at a job you hate because you're too afraid that you won't find anything else, that's not operating in faith; why would your higher power need to show up? If you do the same thing every day, day in and day out, you must be satisfied. Maybe you're content or just settling, but why does God need to show up in a supernatural way if you're content with where you are? But when you make the necessary effort, trust God, believe in him, have faith, declare, and affirm, I guarantee you God will show up in your life. When you build your faith, you eliminate your fear. Do you have faith in yourself? In God? Do you believe things will change? Can you see beyond your current situation?

Energy

Earlier in this book, I spoke about both negative and positive energy. If you take the time and begin to focus on the energy you are transferring to the world, you will see a major difference in your life. Once you've decided that you will only give and receive positive energy, it's up to you to maintain that way of life. When you can control and manage the level of stress, drama, and negativity in your life, trust me, it is pure ecstasy. My personal circle is extremely small. I'm very particular about who I share my energy with. Once you've established a truly balanced life, you will be very cautious of the people and energy you allow into your world.

When you begin to change your energy and the nurture of your spirit, your life will truly transcend and your world will change in a major way. You will begin to operate on a level that is separate from "the world." In 2 Corinthians 6:17, it says, "Come out from among them and be ye separate, touch no unclean thing; and I will receive you." This means that you should not be like everyone else; don't even associate yourself with negativity. When you clean your spirit and walk in the light of positivity, doors will open for you that money can't buy and man can't close. You'll build connections with other pure spirits, creating a network that no organization can recreate. Creatively, your positive energy will ignite innovative and inspiring ideas for success that you've never seen before.

Your energy is everything you are—the way to talk to people, how you treat people, your level of optimism, how you make people feel when they're around you, and so much more. It's not just about walking around saying hello and smiling. It's about how you make people feel without even saying a word to them. There is a stark difference in my presence when I was depressed and angry, to my presence now. We are vessels of the most high. We are God's representatives. So ask yourself, how are you representing your higher power? What energy are you putting out into the universe? How do you make people feel when they are around you?

Karma

It's important that you ask yourself these questions, because what you put out in this world, you will get back. Whether you believe it or not, the law of attraction (the belief that like attracts like) is working in your life. It's up to you to search for understanding and apply it in your life. Everything you do, see, hear, read and say has a direct impact on your behavior, actions, and what comes to you.

So what's karma? Karma is defined as the sum of a person's actions in this and previous states of existence that will decide their fate in a future existence. Again, as I said before, you are the result of the thoughts, actions, choices, and decisions of your past. Whether you want to accept it or not, you get what you put out in life. You are the creator. You are the designer. It is by your hand and mind that you determine what your life experiences will be. Proverbs 23:7 says, "For as a man thinketh in his heart so is he." People have a hard time accepting the fact that they attract whatever they give their attention, energy, and focus to, regardless of whether it's negative or positive. A part of developing a deeper spiritual connection means you accept, understand, and practice good karma.

The Bible has many verses that sing to the tune of karma and the laws of attraction.
- Ecclesiastes 10:8–9 says, "Whoever digs a pit may fall into it…whoever quarries stones may be injured by them."
- Matthew 9:29 reads, "According to your faith, let it be done to you."
- Galatians 6:7 says, "A man reaps what he sows."
- Matthew 12:35 says, "A good man produces good things out of the good stored up in him, and an evil man brings evil things out of the veil stored up in him."

Sometimes you have to take a long, hard look in the mirror and ask yourself the following questions:
- Do I truly believe a higher power exists?
- If not, what's holding me back from believing and connecting?
- Have I allowed room for my higher power to show up?
- Have I challenged myself to be open enough to believe in the unseen?
- Do I have faith? Is it strong?
- Do I provide opportunities for faith to work in my life?
- Could I be stepping out on faith more often?
- Am I bringing positive energy to the world, my friends, my family, and my workplace?
- Am I operating in goodness?
- Is my mind centered on goodness?
- Am I expecting greatness, or am I expecting defeat?

I can't tell you what to believe or how to believe—that's up to you. But just understand that what you believe will dictate your entire life. Your beliefs about religion, spirituality, love, and self-worth are key to how you approach life, live life, and enjoy life. Do you believe that your higher power dwells within you? Do you believe that you can control your mind and emotions so that you aren't ruled by outside circumstances and other individuals? Do you believe you can live a totally free life, filled with love and purpose? Yeah, it all sounded like hoopla to me at first too. However, seven years later after truly diving into all of these life changing lessons, I am living my best life!

So, at least make the effort to believe. Put positive energy out into the world, and know that what you put out into the universe will come right back to you. Get out of the fire! A stronger connection to your higher power will bring clarity. You don't have to suffer or suffocate in the smoke that's clouding your life. I guarantee that, from this moment on if you allow yourself to grow mentally, take charge of your life, hold yourself accountable, become more self-aware, control your emotions, and believe in something greater—something that allows you to see beyond your current situation, you will be in a brand-new place next year. Operate in peace, love, kindness, generosity, abundance, and transformation. And no matter what, live as if you've already won.

12
Brilliant Resilience

There Will Still Be Storms

As I close, I'd like to maintain a level of brutal honesty, the way I have throughout this entire body of work. I've messed up a lot. I've made a lot of bad choices. I've put myself in harmful, dangerous situations. There have been times I've compromised my morals and values. I've stayed in situations when I knew in my heart I didn't belong in them. I've said and done some things I truly regret. But I didn't allow my horrible choices or terrible decisions to consume me. There came a point at which I decided my life was worth so much more, a point at which I discovered God had a calling for my life.

People always ask me how I overcame and how I started over, so I wrote this book. But I don't want you to think I live in some fairy tale now that I have transformed my life. I don't want you to assume that if you do everything in this book, your life will be absolutely perfect, because my life is far from perfect. I still face difficulties, frustrations, and tragedies. I just handle them differently now. I don't allow life to just shove me around. Before, I allowed certain situations to control me; today, I control myself. I'm in charge, prepared, and ready for any challenge that comes my way. Life can be like a battle. Are you scared and cowardly, or are you ready for war? In battle, you have to know yourself (your strengths and weaknesses), be resourceful, take action, and be prepared to win.

You're still going to face obstacles, but if you move toward growth and development, you will be able to handle them differently.

    Obviously, I am still growing, still learning, and still stepping into the woman I'm destined to be. I will always be learning and growing—that's my desire. It takes time, patience, and tenacity to change your entire life around. You will never be exempt from life's trials or from feeling natural raw emotion. You can achieve a new attitude, new outlook, new appearance, get a new job, find a new spouse, or change your geographic location, but with that, also comes new challenges. When you decide to declare greatness over your life, that doesn't exempt you from technical difficulties during a major presentation, family chaos, flat tires, delayed flights, the flu, and the wrong food order. Just because you decide to believe in something different, it doesn't make you invincible. It also won't change how others live their lives or control how they'll respond when you begin to change.

    Not everyone is going to respond with enthusiasm. As I began to grow, I saw people quickly change around me. I was beginning to deal with a different level of jealousy and disdain. I truly love my life, and people feel that energy. But some people hate to see you happier than they are. When I started dating the love of my life, not everyone was thrilled for us. People saw how overjoyed we were together, but that didn't matter. When people are miserable in their own lives, how can they be happy for you? When I finally stepped out on my own and decided not to go back to a nine-to-five, some folks were excited for me, and others could only constantly point out what would surely go wrong for me.

Life will get better and somewhat easier when you learn how to enjoy the moments that matter most. Even in the bad times, you will eventually find comfort in knowing that there is a lesson to be learned. There is always some truth, some light, and some good in the bad times, but only if you believe it and seek it. Otherwise, the bad will just be bad, and who wants that? If you have the option to take the good with the bad, why wouldn't you? Just because we're on a path to greatness doesn't mean we won't encounter storms… it's all about how we deal with the storm.

Standing Strong in the Eye of the Storm
I do a presentation that features how important it is to keep your composure when life decides to kick your butt. In the times when you think you have absolutely no fight left in you, when you feel like you don't have any strength left or tears to cry—hold on and keep going. Keep pushing. It's in the midst of the storm that we learn the most about ourselves, about life, and about those closest to us.

Some storms will be stronger than others, but I assure you, there won't be a storm you can't handle. You have already been equipped with the necessary tools to make it through. It's about recognizing it, owning it, and acting accordingly. Step up and be the person you know deep-down inside you can be. I know you have what it takes to turn things around, because you've made it this far in the book.

Standing strong in the eye of the storm is about building your spiritual core, finding your center, and creating a place of peace within yourself that no one or nothing can penetrate. When you are able to find that centering place of calm, it will help and protect you through any storm. All the things I talked about earlier, like meditating, praying, spending time by yourself, seeking self-awareness, reading, and operating in the fruit of the Spirit, will help build your spiritual core. Your core has to be strong, so strong that when a storm comes it's easy for you to go to your center place for shelter.

When you work out, trainers always talk about the importance of strengthening your core. When you have a strong core physically, it does several things. It helps protect your vital organs, it helps you with balance, and it helps improve your athletic performance. It's the same thing with your spiritual core. When you build a strong spiritual core, you'll be able to protect your mind and body, stay balanced, and improve the way you perform in certain situations. If you stay ready, you don't have to get ready. In the same way that we exercise to strengthen our physical selves, we must exercise to stay healthy mentally, emotionally, and spiritually.

So let's look at the storm. The eye, the center, the core of a storm happens to be the calmest place, where the weather is at its best. The eye of the storm is where you can find the lowest pressure. It's characterized by clear skies, and the wind is extremely light and fair—a thin breeze. In the midst of a strong storm or hurricane, the eye is known to have very little, if any, rain. This is also a place that's known to be a lot warmer than the rest of the storm; it's clear and well defined.

Can you believe that? In a storm, with all that rain, wind, lightning, and destruction, there's peace right in the center of all the madness and chaos. I hope and pray that you can find that peace within yourself the next time you are faced with a storm. I pray that with any negativity, distractions, and disappointments you face in your life, you can block out the storm and truly connect to your inner self; finding peace.

We just talked about the eye of the storm, right? It's in the center, peaceful and calm. Now, just outside of the eye is the eyewall. If for any reason you can't stand strong in the eye of the storm and you allow your faith to waver, you will end up here, risking it all. You will be swept up by frustration, anger, disappointment, grief, depression, fear, doubt, guilt, shame, and sadness. If you don't learn how to create and build that core, stand strong in it, and use it as security when necessary, you will falter. The eyewall is the most dangerous part of the storm. Winds are vicious, moving faster than in any other part of the storm. That's why when you give in to negative emotions or situations it seems like everything comes crashing down in your life—left and right, more bad news, another bad situation, and more uncontrolled emotions. Don't get swept up in the storm. Do your best to remain calm, keep your composure, and deal with emotions and situations as they come.

Unwavering Faith

One of things that gives me great comfort in this world is knowing that everything is going to be okay. But how do I know that? Because I have been practicing unwavering faith for years! Let me break it down. Unwavering means "steady (firmly fixed) or resolute (admirably purposeful, determined)." Faith means "to have complete trust (firm belief in the reliability, truth, or strength of) or confidence (certain)." Those are some powerful words. This means that my faith is firmly fixed, that it's admirably purposeful, and that I am determined in it. You can't excel, reaching your highest potential, with that everyday, old, run-of-the-mill-type of faith. It may get you by, but it's not going to get you to a new level.

Unwavering faith is a requirement for greatness, change, and healing. I know, when you're in the midst of a storm, having faith and believing isn't always easy to do. I had to practice, practice, and practice my faith in order to believe the way I do today. When you've seen the things that I've seen, it can be hard. But faith provides us with that confidence we need to move forward and forget the things of the past. Isaiah 43:18 says, "Forget the former things; do not dwell on the past. See, I am doing a new thing! Now it springs up; do you not perceive it? I am making a way in the wilderness and streams in the wasteland."

Here the scripture is saying to forget about the past. Faith gives us the strength to move on what we believe can be our future. The Lord is saying that he is creating a new life for you, but you can't waver. When you begin to waver, God will look at you and say, "Do you not perceive it?" As if to say, do you not see it? When your life begins to change, it may not always be in the way or time in which you desire. But if you have faith, you will know that he's "making a way in the wilderness and streams in the wasteland." We don't always know his plan or how it's going to pan out. All you need to do is lean on your unwavering faith and stay calm. Romans 8:28 says, "And we know that God causes everything to work together for the good of those who love God and are called according to his purpose for them." So just know as long as you are faithful and believe, the clouds will begin to clear, the storm will begin to disappear, and the sun will begin to shine!

Brilliant Resilience

When you're trying to *Stop, Drop, and Roll,* you have to have a little resilience. In fact, you have to have a lot. You may fall, it will hurt, you may cry, and it may be hard. People will doubt you, and the process of getting over the hump will seem like an eternity at some points. But you will get better, stronger, wiser, happier, and more in tune. You will become more inclined to take on new challenges that will help you grow if you remain resilient! You can't skip the learning and growing process. A new life will cost you your old one, there will be trials. Oprah says, "Where there is no struggle, there is no strength." And trust me, you need strength and resilience to survive the journey to greatness.

You want to go to the next level, right? You want to have the next-level house, the next-level car, the next-level education, the next-level spouse, the next-level faith, and the next-level lifestyle? Well, that next level comes with next-level problems, next-level situations, and next-level circumstances. You have to fight through what you're dealing with now to be prepared to handle what will come next. If you can't make it through this level, what makes you think you can survive the problems of the next level? Patience is key. It's all about learning how to enjoy the ride and respecting each level of success for what it brings to your life.

This ride may bring a lot of detours, roadblocks, and pitfalls, but there's always something to be learned from it—and a hell of a great prize at the end. You have to be able to handle these things with poise, grace, and class. You can't freak out at the sight of every little problem or roadblock. You have to be incredibly persistent about pursuing the life you want in spite of opposition. You have to be able to take some of life's hits. You have to be resilient!

Resilience is all about how you recover from life's blows. It's all about being able to withstand the trauma in your life. It's about not giving up when you feel like you've lost. It's being able to quickly recover and go back to your original state. It's one of those things that will separate you from the rest. But I want you to have brilliant resilience. I want you to face life in a way that no one has ever seen you face it before. I want you to shock the world with the new you!

See, when something is brilliant, it shines. To be brilliant, you have to radiate light and love, and you'd have to be incredibly exceptional. When we see radiance defined, words like emanating, joy, love, health, sending out light, shining brightly, or glowing come up. Being brilliant is all about standing out from the crowd and being quite impressive to others. If you are brilliant, you are probably extremely talented as well. That's what I want from you: talent. I want you to be talented at being resilient! Some of you may have a natural talent for being resilient while others may have to develop it as a skill. Either way, I want you be the best at bouncing back! I want you to shine, letting nothing stop you.

When life presents you with a challenge I want you to handle it with grace and elegance. Learn to refine your problem-solving skills along with your ability to maintain your composure. When you are able to reflect great poise and show the people around you that you are in control, your entire environment and aura and the way people interact with you will change for the better. Brilliant resilience is about letting your light shine for others and handling life in a way that inspires.

A few years ago I was collecting testimonials and there was one in particular that I will never forget. I was extremely proud and knew then brilliant resilience was something worth teaching. It read, "Your motivation has always been my motivation. In spite of all you have been through, you never let them see you sweat, you never give up, and you don't let anyone or anything get in your way...You are always so strong minded and free spirited. You may have struggled, but you live, and you learn." This is what brilliant resilience is all about! You never know who's watching you. We all have a level of influence in someone's life, so it's important for you to let your light shine, and never give up. There are people in your life who need you to succeed. They need to see you triumph. Do it for the ones who are looking up to you, the ones you love. You never know who you will inspire just by living your life. I always encourage people to do their very best, to operate in excellence. Because when our young people, our children, see that we can make it, they are assured that they can too. Let your resilience shine.

When you show people that you can handle life's trials with self-control and intellect, they gain a new level of respect for you. They will begin to see you in a different light. Resilience is having the ability to recover and return to your original state, whereas brilliant resilience is about recovering in such a way that you learn from your adversity, return even better than you were before, and shine your light bright whilst doing so. That kind of strength inspires others to chase their dreams and fight through their problems. This is where you begin to make an even greater impact in your family and in your community.

When you learn how to mentally and spiritually deal with life's misfortunes, you will be free from fear and willing to take more chances. When you learn how to attack your goals in a way that inspires others, you will leave behind an incredible legacy. Don't allow complicated situations, disappointments, and/or learning mistakes ruin your legacy. We all have to be resilient in order to achieve greatness, so why not do it brilliantly? Shine! Inspire others and show the world that nothing will stop you from being great.

Now What?
My Letter to You
  I hope you have enjoyed reading this book as much as I've enjoyed writing it. I'm sure some of you know exactly where you need to start—because a chapter spoke directly to you. Others may feel completely overwhelmed, not knowing where to start or what to implement first. I say prioritize. Figure out where you are and where you want to be. What are your immediate needs? Choose three things and then prioritize them according to urgency. Create an action plan, based off the tools you've gained from this book and find someone who can hold you accountable.

  Do you need to stop procrastinating and focus on execution? Are you buried in negativity? Do you need to drop some of the people, places, and things that are hindering you? Maybe you don't believe you can change and need help developing faith. Whatever it is, the time is now! Choose a chapter and hone in on it. Dedicate some time to an area in which you feel like you need the most help. Keep the book close, stay motivation and encouragement. When you feel like you've made progress in one section, choose another section to work on. I didn't learn all of this in one or two years. To be honest, I'm still learning, still growing, and still trying to practice what I preach every day. It's a process, and it takes time. But I urge you to try something new. Move forward in your life, because there's so much beauty on the other side.

It all starts with you.

God bless. Go leave your mark on this world— peace, light, and love.

Lena

Made in the USA
Columbia, SC
16 April 2018